THE ROLE OF THE FAITH MISSION

A Brazilian Case Study

The cover design depicts the worldwide role of faith missions as well as showing the regional distribution of the faith agencies at work in Brazil. Art work by Cathy Pritchard.

THE ROLE OF
THE FAITH MISSION

A BRAZILIAN CASE STUDY

by Fred E. Edwards

William Carey Library

South Pasadena, California

International Standard Book Number: 0-87808-406-1
Library of Congress Catalog Number: 79-152406

Published by the William Carey Library
533 Hermosa Street
South Pasadena, Calif. 91030
Telephone 213-682-2047

PRINTED IN THE UNITED STATES OF AMERICA

"Christian missionaries should be strategists, expending their strength where populations teem and rivers of world-wide influence have their rise."

F. B. Meyer

CONTENTS

GRAPHS

TABLES

PLATES

FOREWORD

Self-examination is always good for the soul. This is true for the organized group as well as the single individual. Mission societies as well as individual Christians occasionally need to reappraise their objectives and accomplishments.

In recent years such self-examination has been taking place on a wide-scale in the form of research projects evaluating the effectiveness (or ineffectiveness) of Christian Missions overseas. The varied and extensive Church Growth studies in particular have contributed much information as to what makes churches grow or keeps them from growing.

By far the larger share of this research, however, has focused its attention on the work of the traditional or denominational missionary boards. Little attention has been given to the labors of the Faith Missions. This is unfortunate, for these days the inter-denominational or non-denominational societies are playing an increasingly significant and effective role in missionary outreach. Statistics show that one-third of all North American missionary personnel are supplied by these agencies.

We are grateful, therefore, to Mr. Fred Edwards for helping to fill the research gap by making this valuable study of *The Role of the Faith Mission* in our day. He has approached the subject with the courage and honesty of a true objective researcher. Not only does he point out the strengths and advantages of the Faith Missions, but the weaknesses and problems as well. His sole objective in so doing is to enable the Faith Missions to become more effective instruments in the hands of God for world-wide evangelization. This then is something that interests and concerns all of us.

Denominational and Faith missionary societies have much to learn from each other. They should have the courage and humility to do so. Thus not only will missionaries and administra-

tors of the Faith Missions want to consider the findings and
recommendations of Mr. Edwards' research, but those of the denominational boards as well.

As one who has served first under a Faith Mission and then
later under a denominational board, I have a deep appreciation
for both types of agencies. I am grateful to God for any and
all missionary societies that are seeking to fulfill the Great
Commission of our Lord. Especially am I interested in Mr. Edwards' study of the Oriental Missionary Society (known as the
Inter-American Missionary Society in Latin America), since it
was my privilege to serve under its auspices for the first term
of my missionary career. I heartily recommend this publication
to all fellow-laborers in the service of our Lord.

JOHN T. SEAMANDS,
Professor of Christian Missions,
Asbury Theological Seminary,
Wilmore, Kentucky.

PREFACE

The author has been a "faith missionary" and has personally confronted the issue of the proper role of the "faith mission." In a day when mission structures of all kinds are undergoing re-evaluation, it seems reasonable that this particular type of mission be analyzed as well. We yet await a definitive, general and historical treatment, but this study can at least be a preliminary approach to the task.

The pattern of this book is predominantly chronological, and is developed within the framework of church growth methodology. A number of excellent works by Brazilian and foreign authors have been extensively consulted. These are located in the Fuller Theological Seminary Library of Pasadena and the Honnold Library of Claremont, California. The archives of the Church Growth Research in Latin America, the Oriental Missionary Society and the Missions Advanced Research and Communications Center were also used to supply statistical data. The results of the author's "Brazil Missionary Deployment Questionnaire" (see Appendix B) are in evidence throughout the study. Other resources employed include correspondence with mission leaders both in Brazil and at their homeland headquarters, and personal interviews with leaders, missionaries and Brazilian nationals who were participants in the history-making events described in this book.

Acknowledgement is made with gratitude to Donald A. McGavran and Alan R. Tippett for many valuable insights given with respect to church growth theory and research method. J. Edwin Orr and William R. Read provided the inspiration respectively for Chapters 1 and 5. Special appreciation is due Harmon A. Johnson and Ralph D. Winter for their guidance through the various phases of this task. For serving above and beyond the call of duty, I am especially indebted to my wife, Joan, who patiently typed her way through the many drafts.

Hopefully the study will not merely illuminate the past but provide insight into the future. It is also hoped that both missionaries and nationals, both within and without the author's own group, can better plan and work for the growth of the Church through a fuller understanding of the role of the faith mission.

ABBREVIATIONS

AFL	American Federation of Labor
AM	Amazon Mission
AMFG	Air Mail from God Mission
AMS	Armenian Missionary Society
BCM	Bible Conferences and Missions
BF	Bethany Fellowship
BGFM	Brazil Gospel Fellowship Mission
BIM	Brazil Inland Mission
BLI	Bible Literature International
BM	Berean Mission
BMA	Bible Memory Association
CBM	Christian Bible Mission
CC	Campus Crusade
CCF	Christian Children's Fund
CEF	Child Evangelism Fellowship
CGRILA	Church Growth Research in Latin America
CHM	Cleveland Hebrew Mission
CIM	China Inland Mission
CIO	Congress of Industrial Organizations
CL	Co-Laborers
CLC	Christian Literature Crusade
CLM	Christian Life Missions
CWS	Church World Service
EE	Evangelical Enterprises
EFMA	Evangelical Foreign Missions Association
EMCM	*Encyclopedia of Modern Christian Missions*
EQ	Edward's Questionnaire
EUSA	Evangelical Union of South America
FIM	Fellowship of Independent Missions
GFM	Gospel Fellowship Missions
GLINT	Gospel Literature in National Tongues
GYF	Go-Ye Fellowship

HES	Hebrew Evangelization Society
IBJM	International Board of Jewish Missions
IC-YMCA	International Committee of Young Men's Christian Association
IEA	Inter-American Evangelistic Association
IFES	International Fellowship of Evangelical Students
IFM	Independent Faith Mission
IFMA	Interdenominational Foreign Mission Association
IHB	Igreja Holiness do Brasil
IMS	Inter-American Missionary Society
IV	Inter-Varsity Christian Fellowship
JEMS	Japanese Evangelical Missionary Society
JHCB	Japanese Holiness Church of Brazil
LAOS	Laymen's Overseas Service
LC	Literature Crusades
LL	Laubach Literacy
LM	Life Mission
LSEA	Lester Sumrall Evangelistic Association
LWR	Lutheran World Relief
MAF	Missionary Aviation Fellowship
MARC	Missions Advanced Research and Communication Center
MIB	Missionary Information Bureau
MIB D	Missionary Information Bureau Directory of Missions
MIB Q	Missionary Information Bureau Questionnaire
MSWF	Missionary and Soul Winning Fellowship
MTA	Mission to Amazonia
NAPMO	*North American Protestant Ministries Overseas Directory*
NAV	Navigators
NTM	New Tribes Mission
NTMU	New Testament Missionary Union
OC	Overseas Crusades
OMS	Oriental Missionary Society
PF	Pilgrim Fellowship
PTL	Pocket Testament League
SAIM	South American Indian Mission
SAWM	South American and World Mission
SCSM	Southern Cross Scripture Mission
SGA	Slavic Gospel Association
SPAIM	Spanish America Inland Mission
SU	Scripture Union
SWM-ICG	School of World Mission-Institute of Church Growth
TCM	Things to Come Mission
UFM	Unevangelized Fields Mission
UMF	United Missionary Fellowship
UWM	United World Mission
WBT	Wycliffe Bible Translators
WCH	*World Christian Handbook*
WEC	Worldwide Evangelization Crusade
WGC	World Gospel Crusades

WGM	World Gospel Mission
WIM	West Indies Mission
WLF	Word of Life Fellowship
WLC	World Literature Crusade
WM	World Missions
WMC	World Missions to Children
WRMF	World Radio Missionary Fellowship
WVI	World Vision International
WWM	World Wide Missions
WRR	William R. Read
YFCI	Youth for Christ International
YLC	Young Life Campaign
YMCA	Young Men's Christian Association

INTRODUCTION

Faith missions have been so named because of their approach to the problem of personnel and financial support. All of them are theoretically non-denominational in that they welcome workers and support from diverse sources (Lindsell 1962:192,193).

Lindsell indicates that a shift in the support base of the faith missions from Europe to North America took place after 1938 so that by 1962 about 75 per cent of all the Protestant faith missionaries in the world came from North America (1962: 203). He goes on to say that approximately one-third of all North American missionary personnel (8,200 out of about 25,000 in 1962) came from faith sources (1962:208). The *North American Protestant Ministries Overseas Directory - 8th Edition* indicates that more than 32,000 North American Protestant missionaries are serving overseas (1969: Section VIII, 2). If the ratio of faith to denominational missionaries merely held constant from 1962 to 1968, it is safe to estimate that at least 10,000 North American Protestant faith missionaries are now serving overseas.

Nearly a tenth (927) of these faith missionaries are serving in one country--Brazil. There is no single nation with as many North American Protestant missionaries as Brazil, nor is there any other nation with as many North American faith missionaries (*North American Protestant Ministries Overseas Directory* 1968: Section IX, 1-50).

Although North American faith missionaries make up a sizeable block of the total world missionary force, as well as of North American Protestant missionary forces, the investigator is faced with a dearth of information concerning their essential nature and field activity. Thus this study of the role of the faith missions is greatly needed even if the problem is complicated. Because of its large concentration of faith missionaries, Brazil would seem to be an outstanding place in which to examine the role and activity of the faith mission.

The recently published book, *Latin American Church Growth*
(Read, Monterrose, Johnson 1969:58,69), raises serious questions
as to the effectiveness of the faith mission when viewed from
the church growth perspective. It pin-points the fact that
while missionaries serving with faith missions constitute a
sizeable portion of the Protestant missionary community in Latin
America and account for large expenditures of money, their related national churches make up a very small percentage of the
communicant members in the Evangelical movement as a whole.
This is strikingly evident in Brazil.

Just as this study focuses on Brazil for its case study, it
also in Chapter 5 examines in detail the Inter-American Missionary Society (Latin American Division of the Oriental Missionary
Society). This is a successful church-planting faith mission in
a nation where the communicant membership of Evangelical churches is multiplying at more than three times the population growth
rate.

The following, somewhat arbitrary but useful classification
of churches and missions used in *Latin American Church Growth*,
will be employed to distinguish missions and churches according
to the time of their arrival in Brazil and according to their
relation to North American denominational structures:

1) the traditional churches founded by North America-
   based denominations (Presbyterian, Methodist, Congregational, etc.),
2) the indigenous Pentecostal churches,
3) the new missions sponsored by North American denominations, and
4) the interdenominational or "faith" missions (Read,
   Monterroso, Johnson 1969:58).

While this study of the role of faith missions and their
contributions to the Brazilian Evangelical Church is of an in-
troductory nature, it nevertheless sheds light on the activities
of all interdenominational missions moving into the church-
planting ministry. It also speaks to the missionary leaders of
faith missions who are still seeking to find the priority that
best fits God's will and the hard realities of the area where
they are located. It will anticipate for interested leaders
(and explain for those already involved to some degree in the
church-planting task) the tension experienced by the interde-
nominationally-oriented missionary who finds himself being
pressed into working with a national denomination on the field
or the alternative of devoting himself exclusively to interdenominational work and being largely alienated from the national
church. It is hoped that this study will stimulate others to
consider organizational problems and missionary orientation as
possible hinderances to numerical church growth. This preliminary inquiry into the nature and role of the faith mission is
not the last word on the subject. Others must engage in similar
research until every North American faith mission agency is
fully understood by their own administrators, by their supporters and by non-faith missions.

The First Brazilian
Evangelical Awakening

Faith missions are late-comers to the Brazilian scene and for the most part are adolescent children in the Evangelical family of Brazil. No extant North American interdenominational mission agency (the YMCA excepted because of its unique character) entered Brazil before 1914. The faith missions were preceded in their Brazilian missionary endeavor both by traditional denominations and by two notable indigenous Pentecostal churches. In fact, at the turn of this present century Brazilian Evangelicals experienced a spiritual awakening in the course of which were launched the two largest Evangelical churches in Brazil.

THE HISTORICAL BACKDROP

For one to understand the great South American half-continent with her eighteen million people at the turn of this century (Horton 1966:232) and in order to focus on the First Evangelical Awakening in Portuguese America, it is necessary to consider at the outset eight specific events of the preceding century.

Brazil had moved from colony to nationhood on September 7, 1822, and then from slavery to emancipation between the years 1850 and 1888 (Horton 1966:235-237).

In fifteen years (1874-1889) the young nation received 600,000 immigrants from four European nations--Italy, Germany, Spain and Portugal (Horton 1966:236).

The year 1889 is heralded as the birth of the Republic, the United States of Brazil (Finley 1926:386). This, in turn produced two other important events. The first was the loss of the beloved Brazilian Emperor, Dom Pedro II, who was deposed and sent to Portugal. The second was the severance of church-state connections (Latourette 1962:227). Two years later the Republic

adopted a Federal Constitution similar to that of the United
States of America which guaranteed religious liberty (Horton
1966:241).

It was also during "the Nineteenth Century that Protestantism had been introduced mainly by immigration from Germany and
by missions from Great Britain and the United States" (Latourette 1945:166).

The beginning of the twentieth century found the following
missions at work in Brazil:

> Board of Foreign Missions Presbyterian Church U.S.A.
> Board of Missions Methodist Episcopal Church (South)
> "Help for Brazil" Mission
> British and Foreign Bible Society
> Christian and Missionary Alliance
> Foreign Mission Presbyterian Church U.S.A. (South)
> Foreign Mission Board of the Seventh-Day Adventist Church
> Foreign Mission Board Southern Baptist Convention
> International Commission Y.M.C.A.
> Missionary Pence Association
> Mission Society of the Methodist Episcopal Church
> South American Evangelical Mission (Pierson 1901:454).

There began in 1898 what Arthur G. Horton calls, "twelve
years of constructive building of the Republic" (1966:242). It
was during those constructive years that Evangelicalism began
its great leap forward.

The year of the First Brazilian Evangelical Awakening was
1906, in a nation then eighty-four years old. Slavery had been
abolished for a mere eighteen years. The Republic, having
freshly cut its moorings from the Roman Catholic Church, was a
scant seventeen years old. The Constitution guaranteeing religious liberty was in effect for its fifteenth year. The earliest of the 600,000 European immigrants had not yet been in the
country a full generation and were still in the early stages of
adjustment to a new land. There were twelve Protestant missions
and one indigenous Protestant church at work at that time. The
oldest Protestant mission had been in the country forty-seven
years.

When viewed historically in their totality, these changes
give us the backdrop of the mighty acts of God in the First
Twentieth Century Brazilian Evangelical Awakening. This backdrop was made up of two interesting and indivisible parts--the
proclivity of the Brazilian people and leaders to change, and
the social impact of these changes.

THE SOIL PREPARED, THE GOOD SEED SOWN AND THE BARN BUILT

The turn of the present century in Brazil revealed a growing disenchantment with priestcraft and a remarkable receptivity
to the Evangel on the part of the people in general.

In 1902 Episcopal Bishop Lucian Lee Kinsolving declared
that the Roman Catholic Church had repulsed the people by its
unbiblical terms, its services in an unknown tongue, the celi-
bacy of the priests and the confessional (Pierson 1902:145).
This disenchantment with the Roman Church became vocal as could
be seen from an editorial in the *Jornal de Receife* which spoke
of a Bible burning in the state of Pernambuco. A Capuchin Friar
in the presence of 2000 people had burned 214 copies of the Sac-
red Scriptures. The editoral said:

> The time has passed for stifling the human intelligence
> by fire, persecution and violence reminicent of the in-
> quisition which caused so many evils to humanity awaken-
> ing even yet horrors when we call them to mind (Pierson
> 1902:145).

It was Free Masonry, however, that led the revolt of intel-
ligent Brazilians in the matter of the severance of church-state
connections and the popular anti-clerical attitude (Horton 1966:
237). Free Masonry, a mighty force in Brazilian history, had
been an active influence from the reign of Dom Pedro II, Brazil's second and last Emperor, who lent it sympathy and support.
Even though the overall characteristic of this movement of the
intelligencia was secular as opposed to religious, Free Masonry
was apparently God's providential means of opening Brazil and
the Brazilian mind to the gospel message. It gave to the missionary, national pastor, evangelist and teacher freedom to
propagate the "faith once for all delivered unto the saints"
while it also encouraged the people to compare the teachings of
the Roman Church with those of the Bible.

As harvest follows the sowing in things material, so it is
equally true of things spiritual. The receptivity of Brazil in
the early 1900's can best be understood by considering the role
of the Bible Societies and others in distributing the Scriptures.
The British and American Bible Societies were disseminating over
100,000 copies of the Scriptures each year (Pierson 1907:811).
The ground was prepared, the seed was good and the harvest would
come. In 1907 *The Missionary Review of the World* reported, "The
Evangelical workers who are constantly exploring new regions
find that God's word has run before them and large numbers are
eager inquirers" (Pierson 1907:810).

All this activity did not pass unnoticed by Roman Catholic
clergymen. In 1907 a paper in Rio de Janeiro carried an article
written by a monk which denounced in unsparing terms all "American Protestant imposters and Bible Societies" (Pierson 1907:392).

In various parts of the nation signs of unusual receptivity
due to the distribution of the Scriptures could be noted. The
Rev. H. C. Tucker, on a trip in the state of Rio de Janeiro,
found a congregation of fifty people meeting regularly for worship in a building they had constructed for that purpose. The

group had never had a formal pastor and only one or two minis-
terial visits. In places where there was no regular Evangelical work, audiences of hundreds greeted the visiting minister
(Pierson 1907:811).

Such was the fruition; by 1906, the yearly increase of
Evangelicals throughout the country was about 3,000 (Pierson
1907:811).

Not only was the grain heavy on the stalk and the harvest
already under way, but God also had prepared its garner--a spiritually alert Evangelical Church. One such example was reported
by the Rev. S. L. Ginsburg, a missionary of the Southern Baptist
Convention, who told of flourishing Bible classes, prayer meetings, Sunday Schools and many hopeful signs of the great revival
which all were expecting in Pernambuco (Pierson 1906:805). The
pioneers of Brazil Evangelical missions had done their work well.
A foundation had been laid that has stood the test through six
decades of phenomenal church growth. Free Masonry, the Bible
Societies and the young Evangelical Church were the three organizations that God used to prepare the land, sow the seed and
build the granary.

THE AWAKENING YEAR

It is difficult to assess after some sixty years all the
God-directed forces at work in the early part of the century.
Yet, it is clear that God visited His people in Brazil and that
His work prospered in their hands. This awakening is most
clearly seen as we focus attention on the year 1906 and consider
three manifestations that indicate a surge of true Christianity.

The three manifestations of the Evangelical Awakening were
1) the numerical growth of the Evangelical churches, 2) the
deepening of the spiritual life of believers and 3) increased
religious activity.

Church growth was great in rural areas but was not confined
to them. An accelerated growth was felt north and south, from
the Amazon to the Parana rivers. To fully comprehend what happened in the Awakening we must bear in mind that until this date
Evangelical church growth in Brazil was rather unimpressive.
Eliezer dos Sanctos Saraiva, general secretary of the Brazil
Christian Endeavor Society at that time, received reports from
most of the ministers of the Evangelical churches. These reports indicated that there were over 600 new additions to the
churches on confession of faith during the first three months
of 1905 and over 1,350 before July 1, 1905. An estimate for the
entire year 1905 reports 3,000 additions, bringing to 25,000 the
total number of Evangelical communicant members in Brazil (Pierson 1906:199). This forward thrust in church growth which began
in 1905 accelerated in even more rapid momentum in the subsequent years.

The deepening of spiritual life resulting from the Awakening stands out in sharp contrast to what is often the case when a Church grows very rapidly. Often during an influx of members, the moral and spiritual life of the receiving churches suffers a decline (Orr 1967); but Brazil in this period appears to be an exception. Instead of decline "there is an apparent eagerness to more faithfully perform each duty" (Pierson 1906:199). Sunday Schools were crowded with eager scholars seeking a knowledge of the Bible. Preaching services were characterized by the same eagerness for God's Word. In spite of a financial crisis (said to be the worst to date in the history of the nation), money poured into the work of advancing the kingdom in a manner supposed impossible a few years before. Large sums were given to benevolences such as the Evangelical hospitals and Y.M.C.A. buildings. Many churches were not only paying their own pastors but were supporting national evangelists who were being sent far and near to proclaim the saving Word of God to their countrymen. Young men formed gospel teams and reached out into various parts of their cities and towns (Pierson 1906:199). In one southern church several young men published a paper to spread the knowledge of Christ. Another established a church in a state where the Gospel had not previously been preached.

The increased religious activity was in part due to the fact that the churches were fast learning the advantage or organizations and societies to carry on their work. Women's Societies were formed and brought many into the Protestant community. Mr. Saraiva tells of the organization of seventy-five new Christian Endeavor societies and an addition of 2,500 members in three years. These societies played an important role in the training of young workers in many Evangelical churches. Social activities attracted the unchurched. The work of the Y.M.C.A. in Rio de Janeiro spurred the Roman Catholic Church to iniate a similar work.

In all, the year of the Awakening brought a great surge forward in the life and ministry of the Church. Evangelism and a real hunger for the Word of God went hand in hand with social concern and liberality in giving (even in times of financial crisis). The young Evangelical Church in Brazil was on the march. A movement with God was begun that has not been eclipsed to this day.

PENTECOSTALISM'S ADVENT

Simultaneous to the Brazilian Awakening in 1906 a movement began on Azusa Street in Los Angeles, California which spread to other cities and nations. This event has proved to be unparalleled in its significance to the Evangelical cause in Brazil. The Azusa Street revival was not without precedent. There had been a previous, widespread revival in 1858-1859 as well as

local awakenings in Galena, Kansas in 1903 and in Houston, Texas
in 1905. But it is to Azusa Street and this 1906 revival that
Emilo Conde in his *Historia dos Assembleias de Deus no Brasil*
traces the modern Pentecostal movement (1960:11-13). This revival spread to many of the major North American cities with the
city of Chicago being the most effected. A curious but unmis-
takable line runs to the beginnings of two of Brazil's largest
indigenous Evangelical churches, the Assemblies of God Church of
Brazil and the Italian people's movement which was consolidated
as the Christian Congregation of Brazil. The members of the
latter group are identified more popularly as the *"Glorias"*.

From the city of South Bend, Indiana a young Baptist pastor,
Gunnar Vingren, was attracted to Chicago by the news of the revival taking place there. At those meetings he received a deep-
er religious experience which he equated with the Baptism of the
Holy Spirit in the New Testament. It was also in Chicago that
Gunnar Vingren met Daniel Berg, a young man who was to be his
partner in one of the most exciting missionary adventures in the
history of the expansion of Christianity. Both were Swedish and
both had recently experienced a similar Baptism of the Holy
Spirit. As they talked and prayed together, they found God had
given them both a missionary heart (Berg n.d.:29). By means of
a word of prophecy from a third person they received divine direction and knew that they were being sent to Para. But where
was Para? The two went to the library to consult an atlas of
the world. To their amazement they found Para to be one of the
northern states of Brazil. After divine provision to match the
spectacular guidance, the team arrived in Belem, the capital of
Para, on November 5, 1910 (Conde 1960:16). This Brazilian Beth-
lehem was to be the birthplace of the Assemblies of God Church
in Brazil.

The two young men had no salary and worked to support themselves after the Pauline pattern. The churches they founded
were of necessity indigenous. No sending mission and no mission
dollars paid their bills. The message preached was Pentecostal,
as experienced by the two missionaries. The work grew, and Daniel Berg lived to see the Fiftieth Anniversary of the Assemblies
of God Church of Brazil. By 1960 it had 500,000 communicant
members. The church nearly doubled in the following four years,
bringing the communicant membership within 50,000 of the one
million mark (Read 1965:120-121). In 1967 the Assemblies of God
Church of Brazil numbered 1,400,000 communicants. Today it is
the largest Evangelical church in Brazil (Read, Monterroso,
Johnson 1969:65).

Equally interesting is the origin of the Italian people's
movement. In 1909 two men of Italian descent felt led of God to
leave their homes in Chicago, Illinois and go to Argentina.
There they spoke to scattered members of their families and
friends in their mother tongue about the great and glorious
things that had happened in their own lives through the working

of the Holy Spirit in the Pentecostal revival.

On March 8, 1910, they arrived in Sao Paulo where they met an Italian who was a stranger to them, but who invited them to accompany him to his home in Platina, Parana. At that time they did not feel led to accept his invitation but chose to stay and witness in Sao Paulo. However, because their work was not very fruitful, one returned to Buenos Aires and the other, Louis Francescon, went to Platina to visit the new-found friend. Great was his joy on arriving there, for "the Lord opened the hearts of eleven persons who were baptized under the water, confirmed by revelations, cures and manifestations of the Holy Spirit" (Read 1965:22-23).

In the early days they worked only among Italian people since the founder could speak only in Italian.

> The arrival of Louis Francescon was timely, for he was
> able to enter, move, and work in a community of Italians
> that was "in evolution" into their new culture, but at
> the same time receiving new immigrants regularly from
> the old country (Read 1965:24).

Louis Francescon made eleven different trips to Brazil. He was a humble, unassuming person who always stayed with an Italian family that had a small house, many children and a little room just big enough for Senhor Louis to have a bed and a little table. He spent much time in Bible study and prayer and visited church members regularly. He placed no financial burdens upon the young church for any of his physical needs. William Read reports in his book, *New Patterns of Church Growth in Brazil,* that in 1965 Louis Francescon, ninety-six years old and completely blind, was living in Chicago, Illinois. There he had founded another church quite similar to the Congregacao Crista in Brazil. He continued to send regular letters of encouragement to the church in Brazil, which grew from zero in 1910 to 264,020 communicant members in 1962 (Read 1965:25-26), to 500,000 in 1967, making it the second largest Evangelical church in Brazil (Read, Monterroso, Johnson 1969:43,65).

One can draw an illuminating comparison between the Pentecostals in Brazil and the Radical Reformers of Europe in the sixteenth century. History shows that the Reformation had become fettered by state paternalism. Anabaptists and Mennonites like Felix Mantz and Menno Simons took the lead in breaking these chains. In the power of the Holy Spirit they set in motion the hammer of truth which opened the way to a spiritual evangelicalism that flowered in the New World. Similarly, Pentecostalism, in the power of the same Holy Spirit, has freed missions in the twentieth century from the paternalism which shackled the progress of the Church. In simple faith and by using Pauline methods, the earliest Pentecostal missionaries · effectively set about planting churches.

· One will not fail to note excesses in both the European and the Brazilian situations. It is a pity, however, that severe critics tend to concentrate on the unfortunate, but real, deviations from New Testament norms of doctrine and conduct, becoming thus unable to see that in spite of the imperfections "the mighty right arm of God" is at work. Seldom does the overly severe critic ask, "Is this particular situation characteristic of the whole?" or "Is there an underlying validity I have not yet seen?" The unwillingness to recognize God at work in ways not readily acceptable to them may actually hinder missionaries from Evangelical and faith missions from completing their own task of discipling.

THE SUBSEQUENT YEARS

Two example from the years subsequent to 1906 will show the continued growth in that sector of the Evangelical Church now commonly designated "the traditional denominations." The first mission was directed by a North American missionary while the second was a completely indigenous effort.

"Over One Thousand Souls in One Year" is the title given to that section of the autobiography of Rev. S. L. Ginsburg, Southern Baptist missionary, which recounts a year of unusual church growth in the state of Bahia. He said, "1911 will always be remembered as a great and glorious year" (1921:135). Ginsburg invited J. W. Shepard and A. B. Langstom from the Baptist Seminary in Rio de Janeiro to present a "Bible Institute" during a week's special meetings in Bahia. Before the commencement a workers' meeting was held where "One Thousand Souls for Christ" was chosen as the motto for the year. After the "Bible Institute" a three-pronged plan of action was adopted and printed on cards small enough to be carried in a Bible. The plan of action was:

1. To speak to some unsaved soul at least once every day;
2. To pray every day at mid-day for the conversion of some soul to whom we had spoken about his salvation;
3. To give a Bible or New Testament to every neighbor in whose home no Bible or New Testament was to be found (Ginsburg 1921:136).

Ginsburg traveled to almost every church and mission station in the state holding special meetings and organizing forces for the great campaign. He spent the first three months rallying the forces. During the second quarter Ginsburg and his fellow workers went from place to place advising and training others for the campaign. Throughout the months of July, August and September, they held evangelistic services throughout the entire field.

By the end of December of that year, 850 baptisms were reported
as well as the conversion of more than 150 couples who could not
be baptized and accepted into the church because they were not
legally married (Ginsburg 1921:137).

Equally interesting is the story of Anibal Nora (Neves 1955:
29), a young Presbyterian pastor. In 1908 he accepted the challenge of his seminary professor (Ferreira 1959:149) to enter the
valley of the "Rio Doce" which was being rapidly settled by migrants from the arid North and a few hardy German and Swiss families. After ten years' work Anibal Nora reported 1,371 communicant members, six churches, and thirty preaching points. In
1918 alone 139 people were received into church membership by
baptism and profession of faith. This area now comprises the
Minas-Espirito Santo Synod, which is the largest synod of the
Presbyterian Church of Brazil. In 1965 there were more than
30,000 communicant members in this synod, which is one-third of
the total membership of the Presbyterian Church of Brazil. Year
after year the Minas-Espirito Santo Synod reports more profes-
sions of faith than any other (Read 1965:74-75).

RESULTANT GROWTH

In order best to understand the church growth which resulted from the 1906 Brazilian Awakening, we will consider four
Evangelical churches and their growth patterns up to 1930 (see
Graph 1). Two of these are distinct Presbyterian denominations
but because of their common origin, they will be discussed
jointly.

The Baptist Church. At the first Brazilian Baptist convention in 1907, marking twenty-five years of Baptist work in Brazil, 5,000 communicant members were reported (Pierson 1907:146).
In the three years following, the communicant membership doubled. During the decade 1910-1920, the communicant membership
more than doubled growing from 9,939 to 20,135 (Ginsburg 1921:
216-217). The next decade 1920-1930 showed a gain of 17,000 but
fell short by almost 3,000 of doubling its previous membership
(Read 1965:189). For three years following the Year of Awakening (1906), the Baptist Church experienced an unequalled surge
of growth. As many believers were added in those three short
years as in the previous twenty-five. Thus began a steady pattern of growth so that today if all the Pentecostals are grouped
together, the Baptist Church would be the third largest Evangelical church in Brazil, close behind the second place Lutheran
Church, which owes its numerical strength almost entirely to im-
migrating Lutherans from Europe. If the Pentecostals are not
counted as one, the Baptist Church would be the fifth largest,
superseded by the Assemblies of God, Congregacao Cristao no Brasil, Confederation of Independent Pentecostals and the Lutheran
Church.

The Presbyterian Church. The Year of Awakening found the Presbyterian Church in Brazil still smarting from a three-year-old rupture. In 1906 the two Presbyterian denominations accounted for 14,000 communicant members and together were larger than the Baptist, Methodist and Episcopal Churches combined (Pierson 1907:811). The break-away group, the Independent Presbyterian Church, had 4,000 communicant members while the larger body, shortly to become the completely indigenous Presbyterian Church of Brazil, had 10,000. In twenty-four years each trebled its membership. By 1930 the Presbyterian Church of Brazil had 32,000 communicant members and the Independent Presbyterian Church 12,000 (Read 1965:112-113). Thus, in spite of the schism of 1903, both churches experienced steady growth traceable in origin to the 1906 Awakening.

The Assemblies of God. The most unusual growth was exhibited by the Assemblies of God Church, whose founders were products of the awakening in Chicago, Illinois. In nineteen years, from 1911 to 1930, this Church grew from two to 14,000 communicant members (Read 1965:120). In the light of its own subsequent growth, this might seem to have been a slow beginning; but when compared with the traditional churches considered above, this is not the case. After twenty-five years, the Baptist Church had a membership of 5,000 which is slightly better than one-third of the Assemblies of God growth after nineteen years. After forty-seven years the combined size of the Independent Presbyterian and the Presbyterian Church of Brazil was exactly the same as that of the Assemblies of God after nineteen years.

The total Brazilian Evangelical communicant membership in 1906 was 25,000 in a nation of nearly twenty million people (Braga 1929:612). While the Brazilian population grew at the rate of 28 per cent per decade, the Evangelical church membership grew at the rate of 86 per cent per decade indicating that the Evangelical Church communicant membership, to say nothing of the Evangelical community, was growing more than three times as fast as the population (see Graph 1A). The awakened Evangelical Church was on the march.

THE ENTRANCE OF FAITH MISSIONS

When faith missionaries began arriving in Brazil, they typically sensed the foreignness of the Iberian-American culture. Stranger still to them, however, was the large degree of autonomy and the tremendous vitality and growth evident in the churches which had been planted by North American missionaries of the traditional denominations.

Read, Monterroso and Johnson report that "in the early 1930's missions which practiced 'faith principles of support' began to arrive in large numbers" (1969:47) throughout Latin

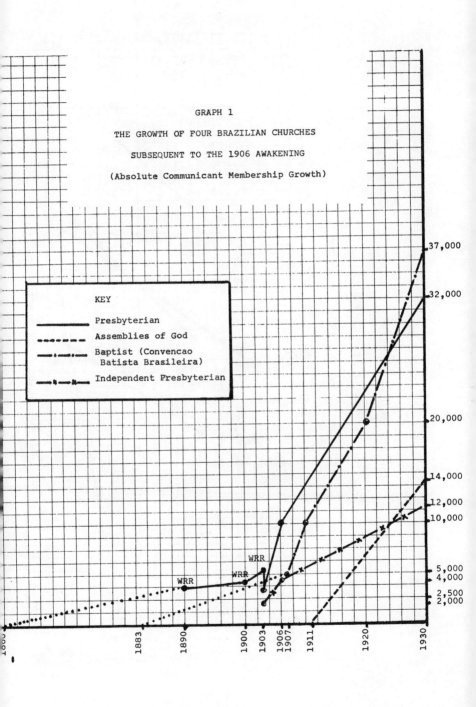

GRAPH 1

THE GROWTH OF FOUR BRAZILIAN CHURCHES

SUBSEQUENT TO THE 1906 AWAKENING

(Absolute Communicant Membership Growth)

KEY

Presbyterian
Assemblies of God
Baptist (Convencao
  Batista Brasileira)
Independent Presbyterian

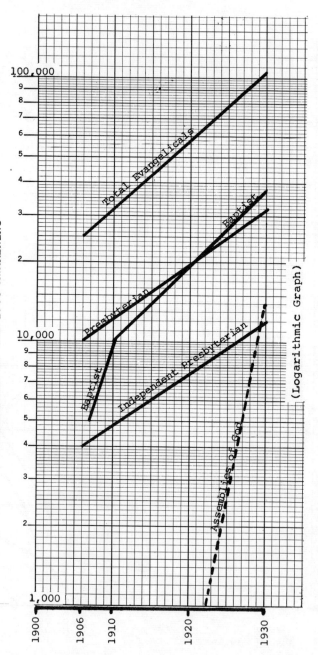

GRAPH 1A

THE COMMUNICANT MEMBERSHIP GROWTH OF

FOUR BRAZILIAN CHURCHES

SUBSEQUENT TO THE 1906 AWAKENING

(Logarithmic Graph)

America. Such was clearly not the case in Brazil. Of the sixty-one North American Protestant faith mission agencies with missionaries in Brazil at the present time, only five entered the country between the years 1914 and 1942.

In 1948 North America-based faith missions began to arrive in force in Brazil. Between the years 1948 and 1968 at least forty-five of these agencies sent missionaries to begin their Brazilian missionary endeavor. Besides these there were also eleven others for which there is no available entry date (see Graph 2).

THE ORIENTATION OF THE FAITH MISSIONARY

We noted that most faith missions entered Brazil in the past twenty-five years. To gain an insight into the unique orientation of the faith missionary, we must study the homeland movements that prepared him for missionary service and sustain him on the foreign field. From what source have such agencies come and why have they multiplied so rapidly? Lindsell attributes the growth of the "faith missions" to three predominant movements at work in the U.S.A.:

> The first is the development of independent churches, the second the rise of the Bible school movement, and the third the development of anti-denominational missionary spirit within denominational churches and among individuals (1962:198).

Lindsell also points out that by 1960 the faith mission movement had produced a constituency of eight million people who were supporting it to the extent of twenty million dollars per year (1962:202).

Imagine the dismay of the faith missionary, converted perhaps in an independent church and trained in an anti-denominational spirit in the homeland, when suddenly confronted with the vigorous Brazilian counterpart of the "apostate" traditional churches at home! There he found people who believed as firmly in the Bible as he did, and who possessed a faith perhaps even more vibrant and living than his own. His bag of weapons cast and honed in the liberal-fundamentalist controversy of North America were suddenly useable only on straw men. Even the missionaries affiliated with the traditional denominations of his own country were largely a different breed from those he had anticipated while still in his homeland. How did he, then, fit into God's work in Brazil? Was his primarily a polemic task? That is, should he carry on a doctrinal war against what might be only imagined inroads of liberalism? Or was his particular task to serve interdenominationally all Evangelical believers and causes wherever he found them? How much could he co-operate with his traditional predecessors? What about the

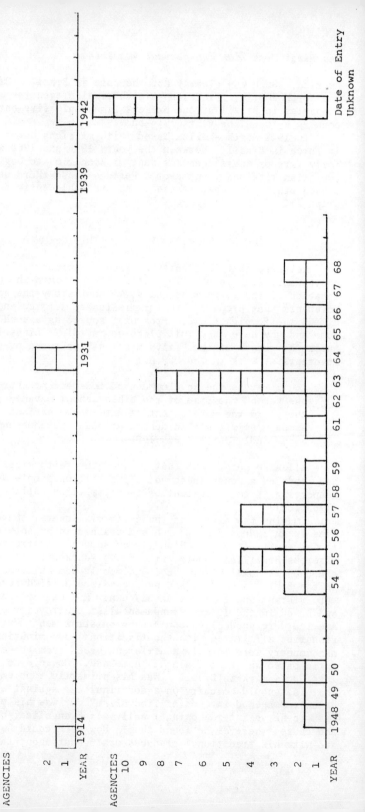

GRAPH 2

DIACHRONIC GRAPH OF THE ENTRY OF NORTH AMERICAN FAITH MISSION AGENCIES

Pentecostals? Were they really Christians? And if Christians, weren't they radicals to be avoided? Should he plant churches? If so, what should be the government and organizational structure of these churches? After all wasn't the *real* Church the invisible body of Christ?

The one thing the faith missionary knew above all else was that his heart burned sincerely for lost men. He must carry the Gospel to them. He must evangelize! Perhaps his greatest and most abiding contribution to the Evangelical Church in Brazil was his impelling drive to use all means (Lindsell 1962:213) to reach every man possible with the good news of salvation. He came at a time when perhaps the bulk of the missionaries of the traditional denominations were preoccupied with institutions of one sort or another (Read, Monterroso, Johnson 1969:46). Thus it seemed that there was a real need for him to involve himself in evangelism.

By 1969 there were sixty-one North American faith missions with 927 missionaries serving in Brazil. These agencies entered the country in two stages. The first five entered between 1914 and 1942 and now account for 25 per cent of the faith missionary force. The second group of forty-five agencies came between 1948 and 1968 and today account for 72 per cent of the North American faith missionary force (see Graph 3).

These faith agencies represent a great diversity of structure and purpose, some comparable with traditional missions, others quite different. In order to more accurately evaluate their work and to learn from them it is desirable to analyze all the North American Protestant agencies at work in Brazil.

GRAPH 3

PERCENTAGE OF FAITH MISSIONARIES SERVING WITH AGENCIES

BY DATE OF ENTRY INTO BRAZIL

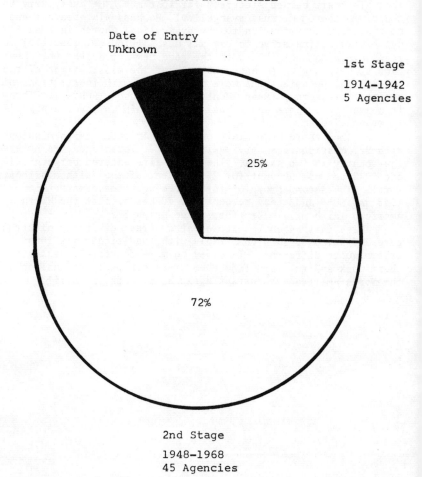

Date of Entry
Unknown

1st Stage
1914-1942
5 Agencies

25%

72%

2nd Stage
1948-1968
45 Agencies

2

The Essential Nature of

Protestant Mission Agencies

The essential nature of the Protestant foreign mission agencies often eludes even the serious researcher. We are all familiar with the popular classification of missions as faith and denominational or as interdenominational (and/or non-denominational) and denominational. These popular terms refer variously to the source of support for missionaries or to the relation of the agency to the existing Protestant denominational structures in the homeland. But they imply little about the work of the mission in its foreign context and do not lend themselves to a quantitative investigation.

What we will call the "essential nature" of any given agency will be described by comparing the home support base or internal structure of the mission with the field activity or external structure of the mission. This type of description of the various agencies requires special research and the creation of a special structural formula.

The following sources were used in the development of the present project:

1) *North American Protestant Ministries Overseas Directory* (NAPMO) 8th Edition: 1968, prepared by The Missionary Research Library in cooperation with Missions Advanced Research and Communication Center.

2) *Protestant Missions in Brazil: MIB/MARC Directory of Non-Catholic Christian Missionary Groups* (MIB D), April 1968, prepared by Missionary Information Bureau, Sao Paulo, Brazil.

3) *Encyclopedia of Modern Christian Missions* (EMCM), 1967, edited by Burton L. Goddard and published by Thomas Nelson and Sons, Camden, New Jersey.

4) *Foreign Mission Board Directory* (IV), December 1967, compiled by the Missionary Department of the Inter-Varsity Christian Fellowship.

5) "Brazil Missionary Personnel Deployment Question-
    naire" (EQ), April 1969, prepared by Fred E.
    Edwards, Jr. (see Appendix B).
6) "First Service Questionnaire" (MIB Q), prepared
    by Missionary Information Bureau, Sao Paulo,
    Brazil with responses from agencies in Brazil
    1964-1968.

The "Brazil Missionary Personnel Deployment Questionnaire,"
prepared by the author, was directed to 140 North American Protestant Mission agencies which theoretically represent the entire
community of North American sending and funding agencies which
have interest or personnel in Brazil. Of these 140 sending,
funding, and non-sending agencies, 124 responded--thus giving a
strong response of 89 per cent. Since the questionnaire was for
the most part directed to the home offices of the North American
sending agencies, the data obtained does not come directly from
Brazil.

In order to compile as complete a list as possible of the
Protestant mission agencies in Brazil, we collated all the
available lists with the exception of that in the *World Christian Handbook* because of its several duplications. The table
included in this chapter lists twenty-nine Asian and European
based missions working in Brazil as well as the 140 North American agencies. Included also is a second list of twenty-seven
groups for which only a Brazil address is known.

Our classification of the North American Protestant missions in Brazil is based on hard data. It is a beginning from
which, with further refinement, application can be made to other
regional and national geographical divisions. Mission agencies
are classified as to the source of their income, their relationship to the existing denominational structure at home and the
actual percentage of their field missionaries involved in ministries that can be characterized as service to other missions or
denominations and/or church planting and development. Now let
us examine the formula itself.

THE STRUCTURAL FORMULA (OR TYPOLOGY) OF MISSION AGENCIES

In the Winter/1969 issue of *Evangelical Missions Quarterly*
in an article entitled "The Anatomy of the Christian Mission,"
Ralph D. Winter proposes as a tentative vocabulary of discussion
the use of two terms: *vertical structures* and *horizontal structures*. Since the two words *vertical* and *horizontal* come from
current discussions of the labor movement, he calls our attention to the distinction between the AFL and CIO:

The AFL consisted primarily of craft unions which, for
example, took in all the carpenters across the United

States, no matter what company employed them, whereas
the CIO felt it was better to organize all the workers
of a single industry, whatever their craft. The craft
unions running horizontally across the whole country,
specializing in a single purpose, were thus *horizontal*
unions. The industry-wide unions, like the United Auto
Workers, which took in all the workers in a given auto-
mobile company, running vertically from the man who
swept the floors clear up to the shop foreman, were in
turn called *vertical* unions (Winter 1969:76-77).

The parallels are plain between the AFL-CIO on the one hand
and the IFMA-EFMA on the other.

The mission agencies of the IFMA (The *Interdenominational*
Foreign Mission Association) run horizontally across
the whole country, and even to other countries, ex-
pressing the concerns of a mission-minded minority within many different Christian denominations. The EFMA
(The Evangelical Foreign Missions Association) on the
other hand, mainly contains mission agencies that express the mission interest of whole denominations
(though of course EFMA includes some horizontal agencies as well, . . .). (Winter 1969:77).

Following Winter's typology in order to classify the various North American Protestant mission agencies in Brazil, we
have analyzed both the internal, home-support structure, and the
structure of the field activity of the same agency. In this
typology the board of foreign missions of a given denomination
which receives its personnel and financial support from within
its own denomination is a *vertical* structure *at home*. This mission may go overseas and set up a *vertical communion,* e.g., a
church denomination. In this sense it is a *vertical-vertical*
mission because its internal support structure is vertical and
its field activity is also vertical. Those mission agencies
that are popularly called the faith missions or interdenominational missions are without exception *horizontal* as to their
home-support structure, since they reach horizontally across a
number of denominations. When such a mission goes overseas it
may, on the one hand, be strictly a service organization such as
Overseas Crusades in Brazil, or, on the other hand, it may establish a denominational church as does the New Tribes Mission in
Brazil. Thus, Overseas Crusades would be a *horizontal-horizon-
tal* mission agency while the New Tribes Mission in Brazil would
be a *horizontal-vertical* agency.

All agencies, in regard to their home-support structure are
either horizontal or vertical. But when the field results are
considered, we must often come to grips with a more complex situation. For example, a mission that is interdenominational

(horizontal) at home with ten missionaries on the field may have
two deployed actively founding churches that will become a new
denomination, two at work in denominational literature, four in
the denominational Bible school and two doing some inter-mission
or interdenominational work. In order accurately to evaluate
such a mission by its field results and to express this quantitative analysis in an empirical formula, we must classify the
deployment of missionary personnel. In the case just cited we
can characterize the mission as horizontal - vertical 80 per
cent, horizontal 20 per cent. In the table this structural formula (one which shows the relation of the home-support structure
to the field-result structure) is written: H - V80%, H20%. So
then, we know at a glance that this is a faith or interdenominational mission in regard to its home structure, but that on the
field it has 80 per cent of its total missionary force deployed
in tasks related to a vertical structure (denomination) while
20 per cent of its missionaries are involved in an inter-mission
or interdenominational work. Note that the formula is always
arranged so that the larger percentage appears first, regardless
of whether it is related to vertical structure or to horizontal
activity.

Another example would be a faith mission (i.e., "horizontal"
at home) which has nine of its ten missionaries involved in service or interdenominational ministries but one missionary who is
devoted to planting churches. Here the structural formula would
read H - H90%, V10%.

To each structural formula is added a list of sources which
will give the reader additional data. The sources are given in
the following, fixed order: NAPMO; MIB D, EMCM, EQ, IV. Where
an agency does not appear in any one or several of these sources,
a blank is left. The Inter-Varsity directory is a relatively
incomplete listing of agencies working in Brazil but does, however, list some agencies that do not appear in other sources.
Therefore, when it is an additional source of information, it is
noted in the resource listings as IV; otherwise, it is omitted
in the listings. For example, the complete formula of the New
Tribes Mission in Brazil reads:

	NAPMO;	MIB D;	EMCM:	EQ
H - V 100%	240;	108';	954;	115

At a glance the structural formula with sources indicates that
this faith mission has all of its Brazil personnel deployed in
work related to its own vertical structure. It shows that additional information is available under listings by entry number:

  240 in the *North American Protestant Ministries Over-
      seas Directory* (NAPMO);
  108 in the *Protestant Missions in Brazil: MIB/MARC
      Directory of Non-Catholic Christian Missionary
      Groups* (MIB D);
  954 in the *Encyclopedia of Modern Christian Missions*
      (EMCM);

EQ 115 shows that this group responded to the "Brazil
Missionary Personnel Deployment Questionnaire"
and the data contained in this response is the
basis of the empirical and structural formula.

In order to gauge the numerical size of each mission, the
total number of missionaries in its Brazilian deployment is
given immediately following the name of the agency. Where a
mission has personnel divided between horizontal and vertical
types of work, the exact number in the breakdown is given in
parenthesis following the number of the total missionary staff.
The number deployed in horizontal-type work is given first and
then those in vertical-type work. The data as to the quantity
and deployment of missionary personnel was obtained primarily
from the author's questionnaire (EQ). At times the MIB Questionnaire supplied otherwise unobtainable data and is indicated
as the source (MIB Q).

The structural formula is based on the data obtained from
the "Brazil Missionary Personnel Deployment Questionnaire" which
was prepared by the author. If data was not available from any
of these sources it was possible in some cases to construct a
formula from other data with the sources indicated.

TABLE 1

FOREIGN MISSION AGENCIES AT WORK IN BRAZIL
WITH A STRUCTURAL FORMULA OF THE NORTH AMERICAN PROTESTANT AGENCIES

Agencies * Asian or European + Non-sending North American x Forwarding for Independents	Total Missionaries	Structural Formula (Horizontal/Vertical) (Sources other than EQ)	Sources			
			NAPMO;	MIBD;	EMCM;	EQ
*1. Acre Gospel Mission	13 (MIBQ)		;	1;		
+2. Agricultural Missions	0	H –	309;	2;	933;	2
3. Air Mail from God Mission	2 (NAPMO)	H – H100% (EMCM)	165;	3;	21;	
*4. Allian-Mission–Barmen	7 (EMCM)	H –	;	4;	37;	
5. Amazon Mission (now dissolved)	0	H –	;	5;	40;	5
6. American Lutheran Church	43	V – V100%	74;	6;	57;	6
*7. Anglican Episcopal Church			;	7;		
8. Apostolic Christian Church	6 (NAPMO)		5;	;		
9. Apostolic Christian Church in the U.S.	5 (MIBQ)		;	8;		
10. Apostolic Church of Oklahoma	10	V – V100%	;	9;	;	10
+11. Armenian Missionary Society	0	H –	381;	;	88;	11
12. Assemblies of God	23	V – V100%	120;	10;	91;	12
+13. Association for Christian Literature (Christian Church field association)	0	V – V100%	317;	11;	104;	13
14. Association of Baptists for World Evangelism	74 (1/73)	V – V99%, H1%	24;	12;	107;	14
15. Baptist Bible Fellowship International	9	V – V100%	25;	13;	121;	15
16. Baptist Faith Missions		V –	;	;	;	
17. Baptist General Conference	18	V – V100%	12;	14;	124;	17 ,IV
18. Baptist International Missions	18	V – V100%	26;	15;	125;	18

19.	Baptist Mid-Missions	98	V - V100%	27;	16;	126;	19
*20.	Baptist Missionary Society	6 (EMCM)		;	17;	127;	
21.	Berean Mission	3	H - V100%	172;	18;	136;	21
22.	Bethany Fellowship	42 (38/4)	H - H91%, V9%	173;	19;	139;	22
23.	Bethany Missionary Association	8 (EMCM)	V - V100% (EMCM)	;	20;	141;	
24.	Bethseda Missions	8	V - V100%	176;	21;	145;	24
25.	Bible Conferences and Missions	2	H - V100%	;	22;	;	25
+26.	Bible Literature International	0	H - H100%	318;	23;	160;	26
27.	Bible Memory Association	1	H - H100%	180;	24;	172;	27
+28.	Billy Graham Evangelistic Association	0	H -	;	25;	181;	28
29.	Brazil Christian Mission	4 (2/2)	V - V50%, H50%	384;	26;	;	29
*30.	Brazil Evangelistic Mission	1 (MIBQ)		;	27;	;	
31.	Brazil Gospel Fellowship Mission	31 (4/27)	H - V87%, H13%	181;	28;	182;	31
32.	Brazil Inland Mission	8	H - V100%	182;	29;	183;	32
33.	Brazil Mission (Church of Christ)			;	30;	;	
*34.	Brazil Mission Within the German Fellowship Deaconry	32 (EMCM)		;	31;	180;	
*35.	Brazilian Bible Mission			;	32;	;	
36.	Brethren Church, National Fellowship (Grace Brethren)	18	V - V100%	40;	33;	185;	36
37.	Campus Crusade	2	H - H100%	183;	;	211a;	37
38.	Child Evangelism Fellowship	9	H - H100%	188;	34;	235;	38
39.	Christian and Missionary Alliance	13	V - V100%	44;	35;	250;	39
40.	Christian Bible Mission	1	H - H100%	;	36;	;	40
41.	Christian Children's Fund	3	H - H100%	386;	37;	255;	41
42.	Christian Church World Missions (Disciples of Christ)			;	38;	;	
43.	Christian Life Missions	2	H - H100%	191;	39;	;	43
44.	Christian Literature Crusade	8	H - H100%	192;	40;	270;	44
45.	Christian Missionary Fellowship (Christian Church)	4 (1/3)	V - V75%, H25%	195;	43;	278;	45

TABLE 1, cont.

	Agencies * Asian or European + Non-sending North American x Forwarding for Independents	Total Missionaries (Horizontal/Vertical) (Sources other than EQ)	Structural Formula	Sources NAPMO	MIBD	EMCM	EQ
46.	Christian Missions in Many Lands (Plymouth Brethren)	24 (MIBQ)	V - V100%	—;	43;	279;	46
47.	Christian Reformed Church	3 (1/2)	V - V67%, H33%	146;	45;	285;	47
48.	Church of God Missionary Board (Anderson, Indiana)	2	V - V100%	49;	46;	309;	48
49.	Church of God World Missions Board (Cleveland, Tennessee)	10	V - V100%	55;	47;	312;	49
50.	Church of God of Prophecy	1	V - V100%	54;	48;	319;	50
51.	Church of the Nazarene	10	V - V100%	117;	49;	326;	51
52.	Church World Service	2	H - H100%	328;	50;	330;	52
53.	Cleveland Hebrew Mission	4	H - H100%	196;	51;	338;	53
54.	Co-Laborers	6 (3/3)	H - H50%, V50%	—;	52;	340;	54
55.	Colonia Evangelica Acailandia			—;	—;	—;	—;
56.	Conservative Baptist Foreign Missionary Society	61 (7/54)	V - V89%, H11%	30;	53;	382;	56
*57.	Deutsche Indianer Pionier Mission	4 (EMCM)		—;	54;	422;	—;
*58.	Dutch Evangelical Reformed Church Mission	12 (MIBQ)		—;	55;	—;	—;
*59.	Dutch Pentecostal Missions			—;	56;	—;	—;
*60.	Elim Missionary Society	2 (EMCM)		—;	57;	461;	—;
*61.	Escole Bibleque				58		
62.	Evangelical Enterprises	11 (3/8)	H - V73%, H27%	203;	59;	—;	62
63.	Evangelical Lutheran Church of Canada (Work under American Lutheran Church)	2	V - V100%	78;	—;	—;	63
64.	(Evangelical) Mennonite Church	36 (½/35½)	V - V99%, H1%	96;	60;	809;	64
65.	Evangelical Union of South America	34 (2/32)	H - V94%, H6%	281;	61;	497;	65

66.	Evangelical United Brethren Church (Now United Methodist Church)	(19)	V - V100%	—	63;	498;	66
67.	Fellowship of Independent Missions	3 (2/1)	H - H67%, V33%	108;	64;	537;	67
68.	Free Methodist Church of North America	9	V - V100%	15;	65;	547;	68
69.	Free Will Baptists, National Association	19	V - V100%	—	—	550;	69
70.	Garr Memorial Church	2	V - V100%	208;	67;	565;	171
*71.	Gnadauer Brazilian Mission	6 (EMCM)		—	68;	576;	—
72.	Go-Ye Fellowship	6	H - H100%	213;	69;	577;	72
73.	Gospel Fellowship Missions	2 (EMCM)	H - H100%	—	70;	583;	73
+74.	Gospel Light Publications (GLINT)	0	H –	—	71;	—	74
*75.	Gospel of Jesus Church Iesu Fukuin Kyddan	5 (EMCM)		—	72;	627;	—
76.	Hebrew Evangelization Society	1	H - H100%	—	73;	606;	76
*77.	Hospital Christian Fellowship			—	74;	—	—
78.	Independent Bible Baptist Missions	4 (EMCM)	V - V100%	33;	75;	639;	78
79.	Independent Faith Mission	4	H - H100% (EMCM)	—	76;	641;	—
80.	Inter-American Evangelical Association			—	77;	—	—
81.	Inter-American Missionary Society (The Oriental Missionary Society)	25 (14/11)	H - H58%, V42%	242;	78;	1038;	81
82.	International Board of Jewish Missions	2	H - H100%	—	79;	667;	82
83.	International Church of the Foursquare Gospel	7 (2/5)	V - V70%, H30%	122;	80;	671;	83
84.	International Committee of YMCA's of U.S. and Canada	1 (NAPMO)	H - H100% (NAPMO)	297;	81;	1423;	84
85.	International Fellowship of Evangelical Students (ABUB)	3 (NAPMO)	H - H100% (MIBQ)	284;	—	674;	—
*86.	Japan Alliance Church	2 (EMCM)		—	83;	972;	—
*87.	Japan Baptist Convention	2 (EMCM)		—	84;	961;	—
*88.	Japan Evangelical Lutheran Church	2 (EMCM)		—	85;	963;	—
*89.	Japan Holiness Church	1 (EMCM)		—	86;	964;	—

TABLE 1, cont.

Agencies
* Asian or European
+ Non-sending North American
x Forwarding for Independents

	Total Missionaries (Horizontal/Vertical) (Sources other than EQ)	Structural Formula	Sources NAPMO;	MIBD;	EMCM;	EQ
90. Japanese Evangelical Missionary Society	1	H – H100%	226;	87;	712;	91
*91. Kirchiches Aussenamt der Evangelischen			___;	88;	;	;
92. Laubach Literacy	1	H – H100%	___;	89;	756;	93
93. Laymen's Overseas Service	1	H – H100%	396;	90;	757;	94
*94. Leipzig Evangelical Lutheran Mission	0	H – H100%	;	91;	500;	;
+95. Lester Sumrall Evangelistic Association	0	H – ___	229;	;	763;	172
96. Life Mission			___;	___;	___;	174
97. Literature Crusades	5	H – V100%	230;	;	;	173
98. Lutheran Church – Missouri Synod	8	V – V100%	81;	92;	778;	96
99. Lutheran World Federation	3	V – H100%	88;	;	788;	98
100. Lutheran World Relief	0	V – H100%	86;	94;	789;	99
*101. Marberger Mission	33 (MIBQ)	V – H100%	;	;	798;	
102. Mennonite Brethren Churches	21 (2/19)	V – V83%, H17%	92;	96;	810;	101
103. Mennonite Central Committee	12	V – H100%	101;	97;	812;	102
104. Mennonite Church, General Conference	2	V – V100%	93;	98;	813;	103
105. United Methodist Church	86 (3/83)	V – V97%, H3%	112;	99;	820;	104
*106. Methodisten-Kirche in Deutchland			___;	100;	;	;
107. Mission to Amazonia (Merged with Evangelical Union of South America)	(9)	H – H100%	;	101;	870;	106
108. Missionary and Soul Winning Fellowship	6	H – V100%	234;	102;	880;	107
109. Missionary Aviation Fellowship	9	H – H100%	235;	103;	881;	108
*110. Missionary Centre of the Reformed Churches in the Netherlands	7 (EMCM)		;	104;	1432;	___
*111. Missionswerk Mitternachtsruf				105;	905;	
112. National Association of Congregational Christian Churches (Work Closed)	0	V – H100%	58;	___;	___;	111

No.	Organization	N	Type	References
113.	Navigators	6	H – H100%	239; 106; 939; 113;
114.	New Testament Missionary Union	10	H – V100%	286; 107; 953; 114;
115.	New Tribes Mission	134	H – V100%	240; 108; 954; 115;
116.	North American Baptist Association	10 (NAPMO)	V – V100% (EMCM)	18; 109; 1003; 116;
117.	North American Baptist General Missionary Society	4	V – V100%	19; 110; 1005; 117;
*118.	Orebro Missionen (Swedish Baptists)	49 (MIBQ)	H – H100%	; 111; ; ;
119.	Overseas Crusades, Inc.	14	H – H100%	245; 112; 1043; 119;
*120.	Peniel Chapel Missionary Society	4 (MIBQ)	V – V100%	; 113; 1055; ;
121.	Pentecostal Assemblies of Canada	8	V – V100%	125; 114; 1057; 121;
122.	Pentecostal Church of Christ	3	V – V100%	; 115; 1059; 122;
123.	Pentecostal Church of God of America	8 (MIBQ)	V – V100% (EMCM)	126; 116; 1060; ;
x124.	Pilgrim Fellowship	4	H – V100%	247; 117; 1076; 124;
125.	Pilgrim Holiness Church	6	V – V100%	130; 118; 1077; 125;
126.	Pocket Testament League	11	H – H100%	248; 120; 1085; ;
127.	Presbyterian Church in the U.S.	142 (6/136)	V – V96%, H4%	135; 121; 1102; 127;
128.	Presbyterian Foreign Missions Independent Board	5 (1/4)	V – V80%, H20%	139; 122; 640; 128;
129.	Protestant Episcopal Church in U.S.A.	10	V – V100%	141; 123; 1109; 129;
130.	Salvation Army	35 (MIBQ)	V – V100%	291; 124; 1144; 130;
131.	Scripture Union	2	H – H100%	; 125; 1174; 131;
132.	Seventh-Day Adventists	56 (EMCM)	V – V100%	3; 126; 1183; 132;IV;
133.	Slavic Gospel Association	8 (MIBQ)	H – V100%	251; 127; 1192; 133;
*134.	Society for Distributing the Holy Scriptures to the Jews	0		; ; 1204; 134;
135.	South American and World Mission	4	H – V100%	253; ; ; ;
136.	South American Indian Mission	20	H – V100%	254; 128; 1222; 136;
137.	Southern Baptist Convention	282 (8/274)	V – V97%, H3%	23; 129; 1230; 137;
138.	Southern Cross Scripture Mission	2 (MIBQ)	H – H100%	; ; ; 138;
139.	Spanish America Inland Mission	4 (1/3)	H – V75%, H25%	; 130; 1237; ;
*140.	Swedish Baptist Union of Finland	2 (EMCM)		; 131; 538; 140;

TABLE 1, cont.

Agencies * Asian or European + Non-sending North American x Forwarding for Independents	Total Missionaries (Horizontal/Vertical) (Sources other than EQ)	Structural Formula	Sources			
			NAPMO;	MIBD;	EMCM;	EQ
*141. Swedish Free Mission (Svenska Fria Missionen – Assembleia de Deus)	19 (EMCM)		___;	132;	1272;	;
142. Things to Come Mission	2	H – V100%	;	;	1300;	143;IV
143. Unevangelized Fields Mission	140 (4/136)	H – V97%, H3%	259;	133;	1313;	144
144. United Church of Canada (Fraternal workers of the Methodist Church–Brazil)	14	V – V100%	152;	135;	1330;	145
145. United Church of Christ	2	V – V100%	153;	136;	1329;	146
146. United Missionary Fellowship (Formerly Pioneer Bible Mission)	6	H – V100%	262;	119;	1081;	148
147. United Missionary Society (Now The Missionary Church)	24 (1/23)	V – V96%, H4%	154;	138;	1342;	147
148. United Missions			;	139;	;	
149. United Pentecostal Church	5	V – V100%	129;	140;	1343;	150
150. United Presbyterian Church in the USA	70 (6/64)	V – V91%, H9%	138;	141;	1344;	151
151. United World Mission	5 (2/3)	H – V60%, H40%	263;	142;	1347;	152
*152. West Amazon Mission	10 (MIBQ)		;	143;	1372;	
153. West Indies Mission	12 (2/10)	H – V84%, H16%	266;	144;	1375;	154
154. Word of Life Fellowship	8	H – H100%	;	145;	1385;	155
155. World Baptist Fellowship Mission Agency	18	V – V100%	35;	146;	1388;	156
+156. World Council of Churches Commission on World Mission	0		;	147;	1393;	157
157. World Gospel Crusades	1	H – H100%	409;	148;	1395;	158
158. World Gospel Mission (Co-operate with United Missionary Society)	(2)	H – V100%	296;	149;	1396;	159
*159. World Gospel Missionary Society	1 (EMCM)		372;	150;	1177;	
+160. World Literature Crusade	0	H – H100%	___;	;	;	161

No.	Agency	Personnel	Ministry				
161.	World Missions	3 (NAPMO)	H - V100% (EMCM)	268;	151;	1403;	163
162.	World Missions to Children	8 (1/7)	H - V88%, H12%	269;	152;	1404;	164
163.	World Radio Missionary Fellowship	2	H - H100%	270;	153;	1407;	165
+164.	World Vision International	0	H - H100%	373;	154;	1411;	166
165.	World Wide Missions	2 (1/1)	H - V50%, H50%	273;	155;	1413;	167
166.	Worldwide Evangelization Crusade	32 (2/30)	H - V94%, H6%	272;	156;	1417;	168
167.	Wycliffe Bible Translators	168	H - H100%	274;	158;	1421;	169
168.	Young Life Campaign	3	H - H100%	___;	161;	___;	
169.	Youth for Christ International	2	H - H100%	276;	162;	1428;	170

AGENCIES WITH ONLY BRAZIL ADDRESSES

1.	Amazon Dental Fellowship		___;	p.15;	___
2.	Assembleia Crista		___;	p.15;	___
3.	Bible Society of Brazil		___;	p.16;	1196;
4.	Brado do Hora Final	10 (MIBQ)	___;	p.16;	___
5.	Brazil Christian Publications (Christian Church)		___;	p.16;	___
6.	Brazilian Baptist Convention, Foreign Mission Board		___;	p.16;	___
7.	Brazilian Evangelical Confederation		___;	p.16;	___
8.	Brazilian Evangelistic Association		___;	p.16;	___
9.	Brethren Assemblies (Plymouth Brethren)		___;	p.17;	___
10.	Christian Literature Advance		___;	p.17;	___
11.	Cruzada do Nova Vida (Rev. Walter Robert McAlister)		___;	p.17;	___
12.	Igreja Evangelica Suica		___;	p.19;	___
13.	Igreja Luterana Independente		___;	p.19;	___
14.	Igreja Reformada		___;	p.19;	___
15.	Imprensa da Fe		___;	p.19;	___
16.	Independent Pentecostal		___;	p.19;	___

TABLE 1, cont.

Agencies * Asian or European + Non-sending North American x Forwarding for Independents	Total Missionaries (Horizontal/Vertical) (Sources other than EQ)	Structural Formula	Sources NAPMO; MIBD; EMCM; EQ
17. Life Ministry			
18. Metropolitan Chapel (Pastor Richard M. Shurtz)		MIBQ 71;	___; p.20; ___; ___;
19. Missao Crista (German Plymouth Brethren)			___; p.20; ___; ___;
20. Missao Evangelico do Interior do Brasil			___; p.21; ___; ___;
21. Missao Mundo Para Cristo			___; p.21; ___; ___;
22. Missionary Union for South America, Evangelical Mission of			___; p.22; ___; ___;
23. Parana Valley Mission			___; p.22; ___; ___;
24. Plymouth Brethren			___; p.22; ___; ___;
25. Sociedade Evangelizadora das Igrejas do Cristo			___; p.23; ___; ___;
26. T. L. Osborn Evangelistic Association			___; p.23; ___; ___;
27. Testemunho Batista para Israel de Sao Paulo			___; p.23; ___; ___;

TOTALS OF NORTH AMERICAN PROTESTANT MISSIONARIES IN BRAZIL

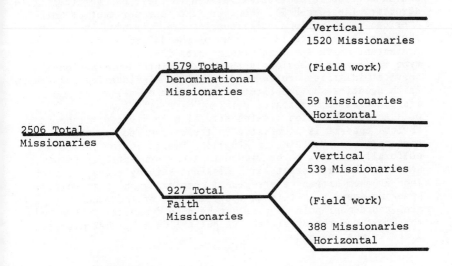

SOME PRELIMINARY OBSERVATIONS CONCERNING
NORTH AMERICAN PROTESTANT MISSIONS IN BRAZIL

There are 2,506 missionaries serving with 111 North American Protestant mission agencies in Brazil. Sixty-three per cent of these missionaries (1,579) serve with fifty denominational agencies. The other 927 missionaries (37 per cent) serve with the sixty-one agencies which have a horizontal home support base --that is, the faith missions.

While 54 per cent of all North American Protestant mission agencies in Brazil are faith missions, only 37 per cent of the total North American Protestant missionary force serve with the faith mission agencies (see Graph 4). Thus the ratio of North American denominational missionaries to North American faith missionaries is almost two to one (1.7 to 1).

Of all North American Protestant missionary personnel in Brazil, 79.5 per cent are in vertical-type field work--that is, related to a national church or denomination. The remaining 20.5 per cent of these missionaries are in horizontal-type activity--that is, they are involved in interdenominational or inter-mission work.

Among the North American faith missionaries in Brazil 58 per cent are involved in vertical-type work. Only 42 per cent of the missionaries serving under the auspices of agencies with a horizontal support base are involved in horizontal-type field work. In vivid contrast with the 58 per cent/42 per cent breakdown of the faith missionaries, a 96 per cent/4 per cent

breakdown is seen for the (North American) denominational missionary force. The 96 per cent work in church planting and
church developing ministries related to their own vertical field
structure (see Graph 5). However, the four per cent of North
American denominational missionaries are fify-nine in number and
therefore constitute 13 per cent of the 447 total number of
Protestant North American missionaries involved in horizontal-
type field work. Obviously the bulk of interdenominational and
service ministries are carried on by 388 missionaries related to
faith agencies who constitute 87 per cent of all North American
missionaries in horizontal work.

     As the Brazilian mission situation is studied, it becomes
obvious that it is simplistic in the extreme to say that a mission agency is "working in Brazil." Brazil is too vast and
culturally complex to be viewed as a uniform entity. Rather, as
we study the Protestant faith missions serving there, we must
look at them within the regional complexity which is Portuguese-
speaking America. It is in the framework of the economic, political and demographic forces that have so dynamically effected
the growth of the Brazilian Evangelical Church, that mission
activity must be understood.

NORTH AMERICAN PROTESTANT MISSIONARY FORCE IN BRAZIL

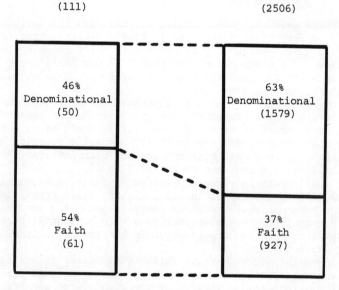

GRAPH 4

GRAPH 5

NATURE OF FIELD WORK OF NORTH AMERICAN

PROTESTANT MISSIONARIES IN BRAZIL

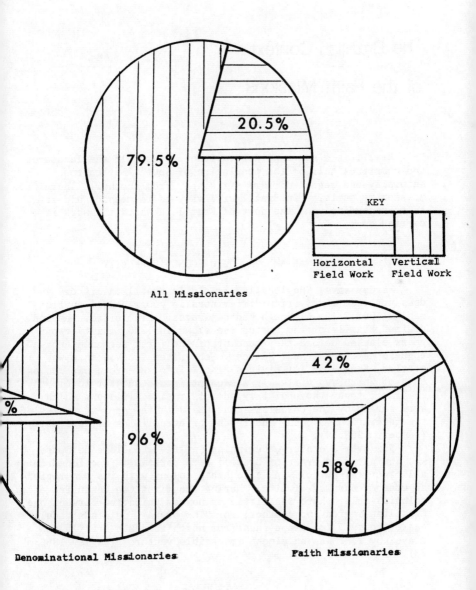

KEY

Horizontal Field Work   Vertical Field Work

All Missionaries

Denominational Missionaries

Faith Missionaries

3

The Brazilian Context

of the Faith Missions

Brazil is a sub-continent. It occupies half the land area and comprises half of the population of South America today. Naturally one region differs strikingly from another. Therefore missionary activity in Brazil will vary as to methods and results depending upon the part of Brazil in which the work is carried on.

REGIONALISM: A SOCIO-ECONOMIC REALITY

Wagley says, "Regionalism is old in Brazilian history and does not rise merely from differences in geographical environment" (1963:28). Although Pedro Alvares Cabral discovered and claimed Brazil for the Portuguese crown in 1500, thirty-two years elapsed before the founding of the first permanent Portuguese settlement near Santos. Soon after Sao Vincente was settled, King Joao III divided Brazil into seventeen *capitanias*, each of which was virtually a separate state subject to Lisbon. In Brazil today the arbitrary administrative divisions which were set up by the colonists continue with the present states of the federation matching the feudal principalities or *capitanias* (Lambert 1967:54).

For over a century, beginning in 1549 when Tome de Sousa was nominated governor of Brazil, each *capitania* functioned for all practical purposes as a separate colony with its own regional economy and way of life. During the first two centuries of colonial rule, there was little or no communication between one Brazilian region and another; for "The prevailing winds made it easier to sail to Europe than from north to south Brazil, and travel by land was an almost impossible venture" (Wagley 1963: 28).

Modern Brazil has six distinct major regions. Each region has its own history and colorful culture, its own distinctive economy and variant climate.

Had it not been for the unique movement of Brazil from colony to independent monarchy and then to republic (in contrast with the other Latin American republics which moved directly from colonial rule to republican independence), current maps of South America would need to be labeled differently. Although the political changes in Brazil came about relatively smoothly and peacefully so that the vast country was able to preserve a unique working unity, none the less a distinct regionalism still exists. Had Brazil followed the same route as her Spanish-speaking neighbors in their movement toward independence, there would undoubtedly be six Portuguese-speaking countries instead of one. But topography and language, coupled with the calm temperament of the Portuguese and their lack of military and administrative strength happily worked against the fragmentation of Brazil.

In the light of her regionalism and yet her unified nationalism, Brazil and the Brazilian are easily misunderstood by the foreign mission agencies working there. For the purpose of planting Evangelical churches and co-operative evangelistic efforts Brazil must be understood and respected as to her regional divisions.

A similar though perhaps not as serious misunderstanding was evident in the case of the year-long evangelistic effort conducted by the Evangelism-in-Depth team of the Latin American Mission in Colombia during 1968. Donald L. Fults, Overseas Crusades' Assistant Field Director in Colombia, reports that Evangelism-in-Depth ignored the regional divisions of Colombia to the detriment of the year-long co-operative evangelistic effort.

> *Colombia is divided into a number of intensely regionalistic areas.* The Rev. Dick Boss, commenting on this said, "Now that Evangelism-in-Depth is working in larger countries than those of Central America, it seems to me that the possibility must be considered of dividing a country as large as Colombia into zones, which can then have simultaneous, although practically independent, movements. *Regionalism was somewhat damaging in the general results of Evangelism-in-Depth in Colombia.*" (1969:2) (Italics mine).

The parallel with Brazil is so obvious that church planting missionaries as well as those involved in co-operative evangelism will do well to take into account its regionalism, both geographical and cultural.

Let us then survey briefly the development of regionalism as it is seen in Brazil's economic and political history from the colonial beginnings to see if by such a study we understand better why some regions of Brazil have been more responsive than others to the establishment and development of the Evangelical Church. In our study we will try especially to discover the past and present role of the North American Protestant faith mission in the planting and development of the Evangelical Church in Brazil. Each mission agency with its Brazilian effort and results can best be understood within its own region or regions.

The Northeast Coast. Plate 1 shows the six distinct regions of contemporary Brazil. The Northeast Coast is the oldest "Brazil", where a flourishing sugar industry and the paternalistic plantation system dominated colonial and imperial Brazil. By the middle of the seventeenth century Brazil's sugar monopoly was broken by competition with the French, English and Dutch in the West Indies, each with its own homeland market. (The technical knowledge of the sugar production was taken to the West Indies by the Jews who fled with the Dutch when they were expelled from Recife.) After 1654 the sugar plantations of the Northeast entered a slow decline.

Nine North American faith missions are currently working in this "oldest Brazil':

Christian Bible Mission
Christian Children's Fund
Christian Literature Crusade
Church World Service
Evangelical Union of South America
Go-Ye Fellowship
International Fellowship of Evangelical Students
Missionary Aviation Fellowship
Unevangelized Fields Mission.

CWS, not a faith mission as such, is included because it is a horizontal agency. Two agencies entered the region between 1914-1942, five between 1945-1959 and two between the years 1961-1968.

The Arid Sertao. Inland from the sugar coast is the Northeast Arid *Sertao*. In this region a grazing economy took form in the days of the sugar plantations to provide meat to feed the slaves and sugar barons of the coast. This "other Northeast", as it has been called , never prospered. Made up of large estates worked by a few *vaqueiros* (northern cowboys) and subsistence farmers, it is today the poverty-problem region of Brazil (Wagley 1963:29).

A total of six North American faith mission agencies are conducting their missionary effort in the "other Northeast":

Brazil Gospel Fellowship Mission
Child Evangelism Fellowship
Evangelical Union of South America
Literature Crusades
Missionary Aviation Fellowship.

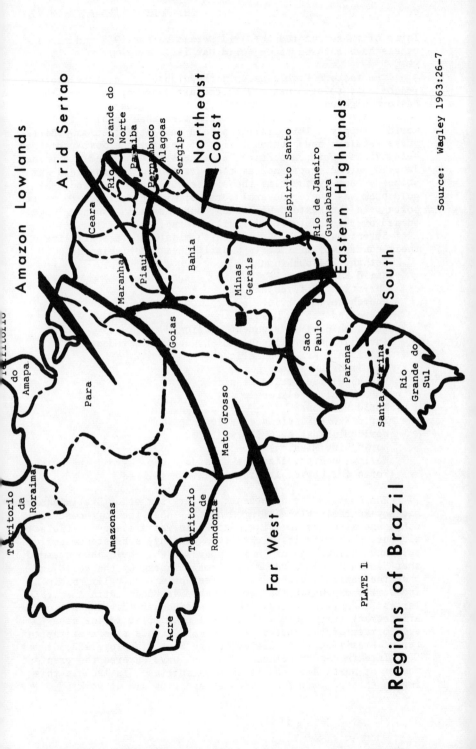

Amazon Lowlands

Arid Sertao

Northeast Coast

Eastern Highlands

South

Far West

Territorio da Roraima

Territorio do Amapa

Para

Amazonas

Acre

Territorio de Rondonia

Mato Grosso

Goias

Maranhao

Piaui

Ceara

Rio Grande do Norte

Paraiba

Pernambuco

Alagoas

Sergipe

Bahia

Minas Gerais

Espirito Santo

Rio de Janeiro

Guanabara

Sao Paulo

Parana

Santa Catarina

Rio Grande do Sul

PLATE 1

Regions of Brazil

Source: Wagley 1963:26-7

Three of these entered the Arid *Sertao* before 1942 and three others have entered since World War II.

The Eastern Highlands. In the eighteenth century another region rose to prominence with the discovery of gold in the Eastern Highlands (east-central mountain region). The gold that poured into Europe from this region more than doubled the world's supply. This Brazilian gold boom attracted many Portuguese settlers and created cities of beauty, the most reknowned being Villa Rica (Ouro Preto, as it was later called). Rio de Janeiro gained importance as the port from which the gold was shipped. But by the time the eighteenth century closed, the gold boom was over. Several forms of mining continue to be important in the Eastern Highlands, but the lands are now largely turned over to pasture and small farming.

Seventeen North American faith missions are fulfilling their concept of mission in Brazil's Eastern Highlands:

Bethany Fellowship
Child Evangelism Fellowship
Christian Children's Fund
Church World Service
Cleveland Hebrew Mission
Fellowship of Independent Missions
International Fellowship of Evangelical Students
Missionary Aviation Fellowship
New Tribes Mission
Unevangelized Fields Mission
Word of Life Fellowship
World Missions
World Radio Missionary Fellowship
World Missions to Children
World Wide Missions
Worldwide Evangelization Crusade
Youth for Christ International.

The South. The nineteenth century saw other Brazilian regions take their place of prominence. When the Northeast sugar coast was rich and thriving, Sao Paulo was a sleepy little settlement which made its living from grazing, subsistence agriculture and the hunting of Indian slaves. Who could have dreamed that Sao Paulo would become the coffee queen of the world and that the capital gained from coffee would eventually enable an industrial expansion that would make Sao Paulo Latin America's largest industrial city? The coffee industry developed a coffee aristocracy comparable with and yet dissimilar to the sugar aristocracy of the Northeast. It was at this time that the center of Brazilian life shifted to the South (Wagley 1963:30).

Into the South between 1914-1968 have entered the greatest number of North American faith missionaries. In 1969 in this region thirty-seven faith mission agencies are at work:

Bethany Fellowship
Bible Conferences and Missions
Bible Memory Association
Campus Crusade
Child Evangelism Fellowship
Christian Children's Fund
Christian Life Missions
Christian Literature Crusade
Cleveland Hebrew Mission
Co-Laborers
Evangelical Enterprises
Fellowship of Independent Missions
Go-Ye Fellowship
Hebrew Evangelization Society
Inter-American Missionary Society
International Fellowship of Evangelical Students
Japanese Evangelical Missionary Society
Laubach Literacy
Missionary and Soul Winning Fellowship
Navigators
New Testament Missionary Union
New Tribes Mission
Overseas Crusades
Scripture Union
Slavic Gospel Association
Spanish American Inland Mission
Things to Come Mission
United Missionary Fellowship
United World Missions
West Indies Mission
Word of Life Fellowship
World Gospel Crusades
World Gospel Mission
World Radio Missionary Fellowship
Worldwide Evangelization Crusade
World Wide Missions
Young Life Campaign.

The extreme South developed a cattle industry to feed the coffee *fazendas* of Sao Paulo as also had the Arid Northeast to feed the sugar barons. Rio Grande do Sul had had a grazing economy from very early times but it had only been a hide-selling industry until the Sao Paulo market developed. In between the southern region of the great cattle *estancias* was an area of mountains and araucaria pines. Into this area in the later nineteenth century flocked Germans, Italians and Poles. They attempted the mixed-farming way of life that they had known in Europe. In this mixed-farming, grain was planted for the animals and each family produced its own meat, fruits, cereals, and vegetables.

The Amazon Lowlands. One can readily trace the major regions of the country by following the economic booms of Brazil --from sugar to gold to coffee; then in the latter part of the nineteenth century and at the beginning of this century, there followed the rubber boom in the Amazon Lowlands. Hundreds of thousands of people from the drought-stricken Northeast sought their fortunes in the rubber forests of the Amazon. Great cities arose at Belem and Manaus. Ocean steamers moved up the Amazon River to load rubber for the United States and Europe. But this boom was to be short lived. New plantations of the Far East, which could produce rubber superior in quality to that of Brazil, came into full production in 1913; and the Amazon rubber boom was over (Wagley 1963:31).

Seven of the North America based faith missions have personnel deployed in the Amazon Lowlands:

Amazon Mission
Evangelical Union of South America
International Fellowship of Evangelical Students
Missionary Aviation Fellowship
New Testament Missionary Union
New Tribes Mission
Unevangelized Fields Mission.

While during the latter nineteenth and early twentieth centuries there were also minor economic booms creating their own sub-regions (such as long-fiber cotton in the arid Northeast and cacao in southern Bahia), the next great economic cycle was industrial. The coffee capital grew as the land became exhausted and *fazendeiros* moved westward in the state of Sao Paulo and south to the state of Parana. Coffee capital was the financial base of the industrial expansion that has today made Sao Paulo an industrial giant. Because of the prosperity of the South in general and Sao Paulo in particular, the *paulista* tends to regard himself as the supporter of the whole nation.

Egydio do Camara Souza, Director of Brazilian Government Trade Bureau under Getulio Vargas in 1944 while inviting an "unselfish participation" of United States' capital in Brazil's economic future, expressed the determination of his country to industrialize: ". . . Brazil will be industrialized. . . That is the solemn promise of the present government to our generation" (Souza 1944:6).

Brazil as compared to her Latin American neighbors has a high level of economic and social development. Yet this is not the whole story and we can not settle for so simple a view of its socio-economic development. Lambert classifies Brazil as an unevenly developed country and points to the fact that as late as 1960 twenty-five or thirty million of Brazil's seventy million inhabitants living in the southern states and in large cities all over the country belonged to a developed organized society. The balance still retain the traits of an archaic culture that vanished from Western Europe several centuries ago (1967:44).

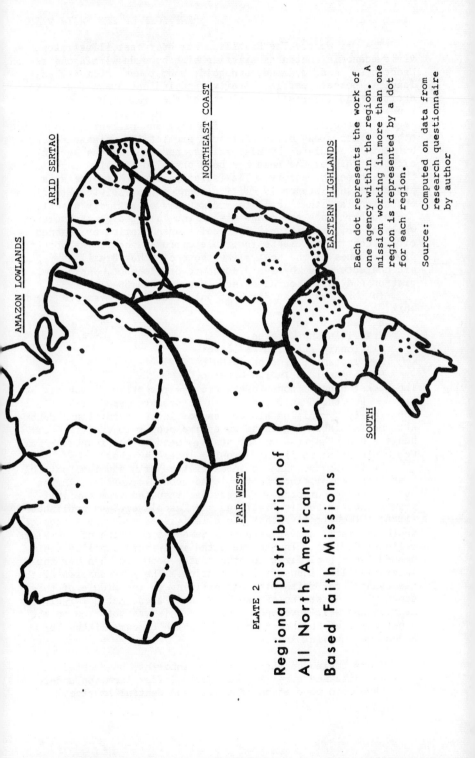

AMAZON LOWLANDS

ARID SERTAO

NORTHEAST COAST

EASTERN HIGHLANDS

Each dot represents the work of
one agency within the region. A
mission working in more than one
region is represented by a dot
for each region.

Source: Computed on data from
research questionnaire
by author

SOUTH

FAR WEST

PLATE 2

Regional Distribution of
All North American
Based Faith Missions

The Far West. The Brazilian Far West best illustrates
vivid economic contrasts existing side by side within one region.
Unoccupied land, diamonds and gold, boom towns, self-styled
leaders, posses, cattle, poverty, and Indians are a few of the
exciting and colorful ingredients of the Brazilian West. A distinction needs to be made between the semi-occupied land of this
region on the one hand and the frontier and pioneer zones on the
other. Vast areas of the Far West are totally uninhabited or
but thinly populated by pastoralists and subsistence agricultur-
alists. Much of the West has been occupied in this manner since
the seventeenth century. The isolation of much of the area is
profound; subsistence is difficult and social services (medicine,
education, and the like) are rudimentary or entirely absent.
The pioneer zones are found within the larger area as enclaves
wherever soil conditions, lines of transportation or planned
cities combine to create favorable circumstances. The pocket
pioneer zones of the West, like those of other Brazilian regions,
are characterized by rapid economic development, rapid immigration and rapid social change (Wagley 1963:88-91).

In this Brazilian Far West only five faith missions are at
work:

Berean Mission
Brazil Inland Mission
Missionary Aviation Fellowship
New Testament Missionary Union
South American Indian Mission.

The pocket pioneer zones are where the receptive people are located. Let the Evangelical faith missionary heed this God-given
opportunity by joining his colleagues in the traditional denom-
nations in discipling these receptive people to Christ. Here
hangs a heavy harvest on the stalk. Send in the reapers! Gar-
ner God's grain in living, growing local churches.

It is not too much to speak of the North and the South of
Brazil as two distinct cultural and economic worlds. In the
South a heavy European influence has resulted from the immigrants who arrived in Brazil as soon as slavery was abolished
(1888). Lambert says that these immigrants made the states of
southern Brazil almost as purely European as those of the Plata
region (1967:41). In Sao Paulo the immigrants supplied the
needed labor pool first for the coffee boom and then for the
later Brazilian industrial revolution. The missionaries of the
new Evangelical faith missions arriving in the middle of this
century in the states of Sao Paulo and Parana met a largely receptive and well-developed society. This was not true in the
other world of Northeastern Brazil which Lambert likens to
Andean and Central America.

There living conditions of the ignorant, uneducated
and diseased rural masses hardly differ from the underdeveloped population of Andean and Central America.

Fecundity is equally high, life expectancy and per
capita income as low, and illiteracy equally wide
spread. . . (1967:45).

Those Evangelical faith missions that entered and located
in the North of Brazil found themselves working in a very different situation: it was an underdeveloped society which was
largely resistant to their message and purpose.

REGIONALISM: A POLITICO-HISTORICAL FACT

The locus of political power moved geographically along the
route of the economic development in Brazil which we have just
viewed. The political struggle of imperial and independent
Brazil (1822-1887) after 1836 is described by Brazil's great
foreign minister, Baron de Rio Branco, as a struggle of two parties, the conservative and the liberal. During this time Dom
Pedro II, the Emperor of independent Brazil sided increasingly
with the liberal party. Fernando de Azevedo says he thus em-
barked on a course of "dynastic suicide." First he alienated
himself from the twin powers of the Roman Catholic Church and
the military, and later from the landed aristocracy of the Northeast. Azevedo thinks that Pedro II failed to understand that
the plantation aristocracy of the sugar coast was the financial
base of the Brazilian Empire (1950:105). It seems doubtful that
this could be the case for such a wise and benign ruler with an
obvious love for his people. It is far more reasonable to pre-
sume that Dom Pedro II was, as are all men to some large degree,
a child of his times. He drank deeply of the wells of French
positivism and of the republicanism of his day that was fanned
by breezes from the United States example. This fact is at-
tested to by his support of the Freemasons against the Roman
Catholic Church. Pedro II was a liberal Emperor--a strange
hybrid when viewed from our standpoint--but a product of his
time.
    Brazil alone among the Latin American republics moved not
from colony to republic but from an independent monarchy to republic. This is a fact worth remembering.
    The Northeast aristocracy which had already felt the slip-
page of their economic and political power due to the dominance
of the metals in the Eastern Highlands, received what was virtually a *coup de grace* when the Regent Princess Isabel signed the
decree of total abolition of slavery in May, 1888. The shortage
of cheap labor which resulted served to undermine the economic
foundations of the Empire. The military and the religious sup-
ports had already been lost to the Brazilian Empire. On November 15, 1889, Brazil was declared to be the Republic of the
United States of Brazil with the Imperial family's sailing to
Portugal (Yuasa 1967:5).

The Brazilian cultural historian, Azevedo, says:

The second Brazilian Empire represented in the political
evolution an effort at unification, sufficient for the
Republic to begin without the twin perils of fragmentation and of caudillism (1950:106).

To understand this tension between republicanism and centralization of power is to understand Brazil's political history and
the large role of the military, particularly the army which
views itself as custodian of the Republic. It continues to be
a conservative force favoring centralization.

During these early days of the Republic and in the early
years of the twentieth century just prior to the coffee crisis,
the center of political as well as economic power inevitably
moved further south to Sao Paulo. It is not incidental to the
Brazilian political scene that the states of Minas Gerais (the
scene of the Brazilian gold rush) and Sao Paulo (the region of
the coffee-industrial booms) have become the political powers
of modern Brazil with the states to their north and south respectively lining up behind them. The presidents of the Republic have (with a few disruptive interruptions) been alternately
paulistas and *mineiros*.

The Republic's Stormy Beginning. The student of Brazilian
political history finds it no placid pool into which he can gaze.
Brazil's republican beginnings can be best described as tempes-
tuous except when compared to other Latin American republics.
As we said above, from the founding of the Republic the army has
played a large and often dominant role in Brazilian political
life. Horton says, "The army, not the common man, established
the republic" (1966:241). During the last days of the Brazilian
Empire Dom Pedro II found himself alienated from the army for
two reasons. He tried to eliminate politics from the armed services (which feat has not been accomplished to date) and the
army felt neglected because of Pedro's liberalism (Horton 1966:
237).

Deodoro de Fonseca headed the provisional government as the
first president of the United States of Brazil with a military
man, Marshal Floriano Peixote, as vice president. Fonseca, after decreeing universal manhood suffrage, separation of church
and state, freedom of religion, a new civil code and seculari-
zation of the cemeteries, quarreled with Congress. Then on
November 3, 1891, he dissolved Congress and assumed dictatorial
powers.

Shortly afterwards Fonseca resigned and was succeeded by
Vice President Peixote. Perhaps President Peixote could best be
described as an opportunistic general. When thirteen generals
demanded Peixote's resignation, they were jailed. Then the Brazilian navy revolted; and with the warships of the United States,

Great Britain, France, Italy and Portugal all in Brazilian
waters, Peixote crushed the revolt and followed it with a reign
of terror (Horton 1966:241).
   In 1894 Pradato Jose de Morais Barros, an able lawyer from
Sao Paulo, succeeded to the presidency. The economy was at a
low ebb and Barros was caught between the feuding army and navy.

   Twelve Constructive Years (1898-1910). The early stormy
years of the Brazilian Republic were followed by twelve years
of constructive building of the Republic. Brazil's fourth president was also a *paulista* named Manuel de Campos Salles. Prosperity was restored to the young republic by a huge loan from
the House of Rothschild and the strong beginnings of the rubber
and coffee booms of the Amazon Lowlands and Sao Paulo.
   Dr. Francisco de Paulo Rodriques, Brazil's fifth president,
put Brazil on the gold standard. Coffee and rubber exports were
at a new time high. Economic life was looking up.
   Alfonso Penna (1906-1909) from the state of Minas Gerais
became the sixth president of Brazil and closed the constructive
period. The three great Brazilian statesmen of this period were
Baron de Rio Branco, Joaquim Nabuco and Rui Barbosa.
   Quite significantly it was during these constructive years
that Brazilian Evangelicals experienced their First Evangelical
Awakening described in Chapter 1. However, these years stand
in stark contrast with the next period of Brazilian political
history. Not in peace but in turmoil the first of the existing
North America-based faith missions entered the country (the
South American Indian Mission).

   Brazil's Period of Turmoil (1910-1930). In 1910, 90 per
cent of the rubber and 75 per cent of the world's coffee came
from Brazil. In this same year Hermes da Fonseca, nephew of
Brazil's first president, was the army's candidate for the presidency. He was opposed by liberal Rui Barbosa. Fonseca won
and the large role played by the army in Brazilian politics was
highlighted by the manipulation of elections, bargains with
political bosses and battles with the navy with reprisals by the
clube militar (Horton 1966:242).
   The shifting alliances between local political machines and
party chieftains were dominated at this time by the states of
Sao Paulo and Minas Gerais. These two states between themselves
furnished all but two of the presidents during the first forty
years of the Republic (1889-1930). The states of Sao Paulo and
Minas Gerais became so powerful that at times each had militias
which were larger than the army of the federal government. During this time the strength of the states' rights concept of republicanism was seen when Sao Paulo made trade treaties unila-
terally with foreign governments for the export of coffee without any reference to the Brazilian federal government.
   The rubber bonanza in the Amazon collapsed. Brazil's

income from rubber dropped from 124,000,000 dollars in 1910 to
5,000,000 dollars in 1921 (Horton 1966:243).

By 1910 the coffee industry also was in trouble. In 1870
Brazil sold 50 per cent of the world's coffee and 75 per cent by
1910. Sao Paulo with rich, red soil, with expert foreign agricultural techniques and complete disregard to world competition,
produced twenty million bags of 132 pounds each in 1906, an
amount almost equal to the total world consumption in that year.
Overproduction, competition and falling prices seriously im-
paired the coffee market by 1910.

Wenceslaw Bras Pereira Gomes was president during World War
I. Brazilian exports in 1914 fell to about 50 per cent of that
of the previous year. Bras' administration imposed higher taxes,
cut the national budget, and stressed economy by public offi-
cials; nevertheless Bras was forced to default on the national
budget and began to issue printing press money.

Because of her heavy European population loyalties were divided concerning World War I. At first she maintained her neu-
trality; then in October, 1917, Brazil became the only South
American country to declare war on Germany. The war years (1915-
1917) brought a temporary prosperity to Brazil.

Epitacio da Silva Pessoa was the ninth president during a
stormy post-war period.

The administration of President Artur da Silva Bernardes
(1922-1926) was confronted with the problems of dissident army
elements led by ex-President Hermes da Fonseca and the birth of
the Communist Party in Brazil encouraged by poverty, disease and
the remnants of the feudal system.

It was President Washington Luiz Pereira Souza (1926-1930)
with an able cabinet who led Brazil in a brief upturn to prosperity. Usually in Brazil political power has emanated from
those places where the economic lights shone brightest. The
Brazilian Republic has stood under the large shadow of the Brazilian army whose influence was idealized as always benevolent
but was in fact at times opportunistic. Throughout the history
of the Republic from its inception until the Souza administration the pendulum of Brazilian politics kept swinging from
strong central control to extreme states' rights.

The New Era and Vargas. Until 1930 there was a distinct
elite which directed the destinies of the country. The same
great land holders who dominated affairs in the Empire continued
to do so throughout the Republic.

During the 1930's this time-honored imbalance began to
break down and new political factors entered the scene. One
such factor was created by the Brazilian-born children of immigrants. The descendants of the immigrants were adapting themselves to life in the Brazilian setting but they were not willing to adapt to the feudal clan system of the landed elite
(Yuasa 1968:10). As these new Brazilians prospered economically,
their influence increased proportionately.

In the cities the industrial "proletariat" increased in
size and political importance. In the rural areas large land
holdings were in the process of being divided and sold. Although the vastly larger portion of the land remained in the
hands of the few, the number of property owners significantly
increased in the 1930's.

For instance, in the state of Sao Paulo in 1930 there
were 110,975 individual properties recorded. Only four
years later this number had more than doubled to 274,740
(Yuasa 1968:10).

These sociological changes in city and country tended to
diminish the power of the traditional elite especially in the
South where political power was strongest. Here is a partial
explanation of the political conflicts of the early 1930's and
the coming to power of Getulio Vargas in 1934 with the support
of these forces.

Key Yuasa demonstrates the shift of political power from
the elite and middle class parties to the labor party as re-
flected in the composition of the Federal Congress between 1945
and 1962.

Percentage of seats in the Federal Congress by parties:

Year	PSD	UDN	PTB
1945	53%	27%	8%
1954	35%	23%	16%
1962	30%	23%	27%

PSD: Social Democratic Party   UDN: National Democratic
PTB: Brazilian Labor Party.   Union

The above figures indicate a drastic decrease in the influence
of the PSD which was supported mainly by the rural upper and
middle classes. The UDN, partly rural but also supported by the
urban middle class, seems to have compensated for its rural
losses with urban middle gain; hence, it largely held its own
but shows some decrease. The PTB received support from the
growing urban working class and from the sub-proletariat (1968:
11).

It is in the dictatorship of Getulio Vargas (1930-1945)
that we see the extreme swing to strong central political power
but with one distinction. Vargas was in step with the aspira-
tion of the people and received his mandate to govern not from
the traditional forces but from the new forces of the urban
working class and the new small land owners of the South. He
had been governor of the state of Rio Grande do Sul. He assumed
the executive power as dictator and held that power for fifteen
years when in a bloodless coup the army ousted him. Probably no
other Brazilian politician so perfectly personified *o patron*
(the idealized father figure of the landed aristocracy of the
Northeast).

The new forces at work in Brazil prior to and throughout

the first Vargas administration (1930-1945)--the diminishing power of the traditional elite, the rise of the urban working class and the new small land owner in the South and Eastern Highlands regions--created a new receptivity and provided an unparalleled opportunity for the four North American faith missions that entered and began their Brazilian effort during that time (Evangelical Union of South America, Unevangelized Fields Mission, Brazil Gospel Fellowship Mission and Child Evangelism Fellowship). These agencies worked in all the Brazilian regions, with the exception of the Far West. They met a people in the process of change, in an economic upward movement and within a politically stable environment. Large numbers of Brazilians shaped by the new forces of the Vargas era were ready to listen to the Gospel, believe Christ and accept the Protestant ethic. Nowhere was the new receptivity as pronounced as in the regions of the South and the Eastern Highlands.

Major General Eurico Gaspar Dutra of the Social Democratic Party won the presidency by a large majority in 1945. A new constitution was adopted in 1946 and the Communist Party was declared illegal in May 1947. Revolutionary attempts by the Communists in 1949 and 1950 were both unsuccessful.

Then in 1950 former President Vargas won the election by a plurality. He was backed by a coalition of the Brazilian Labor Party and the Social Progressive Party. But his task seemed hopeless, and his every effort opposed by powerful and dark forces. He committed suicide on August 24, 1954.

The Vargas mystique lives on to the present as the pendulum from central to state power continues to swing; the shadow of army dominance in the political life of the nation lengthens while the patience of military men with civilian politicians and political systems grows shorter. The locus of political power continues to reside in the states of Sao Paulo and Minas Gerais.

It has been in these last two decades that the bulk of the North American faith mission agencies (forty-four have entered Brazil and are seeking to fulfill their concept of mission (see Graph 6).

POPULATION: THE VITAL REVOLUTION

The United Nations reports the population of the world at the time of Christ to have been between 200 million and 300 million. By A. D. 1650 the population of the world had probably risen to about 545 million. Since that date there has been a continuous acceleration. The most recent official estimate of the United Nations gives the recorded average annual rate of world population growth (from 1958-1964) at seventeen per thousand.

GRAPH 6

Brazil Entry of North America-Based Faith Missions

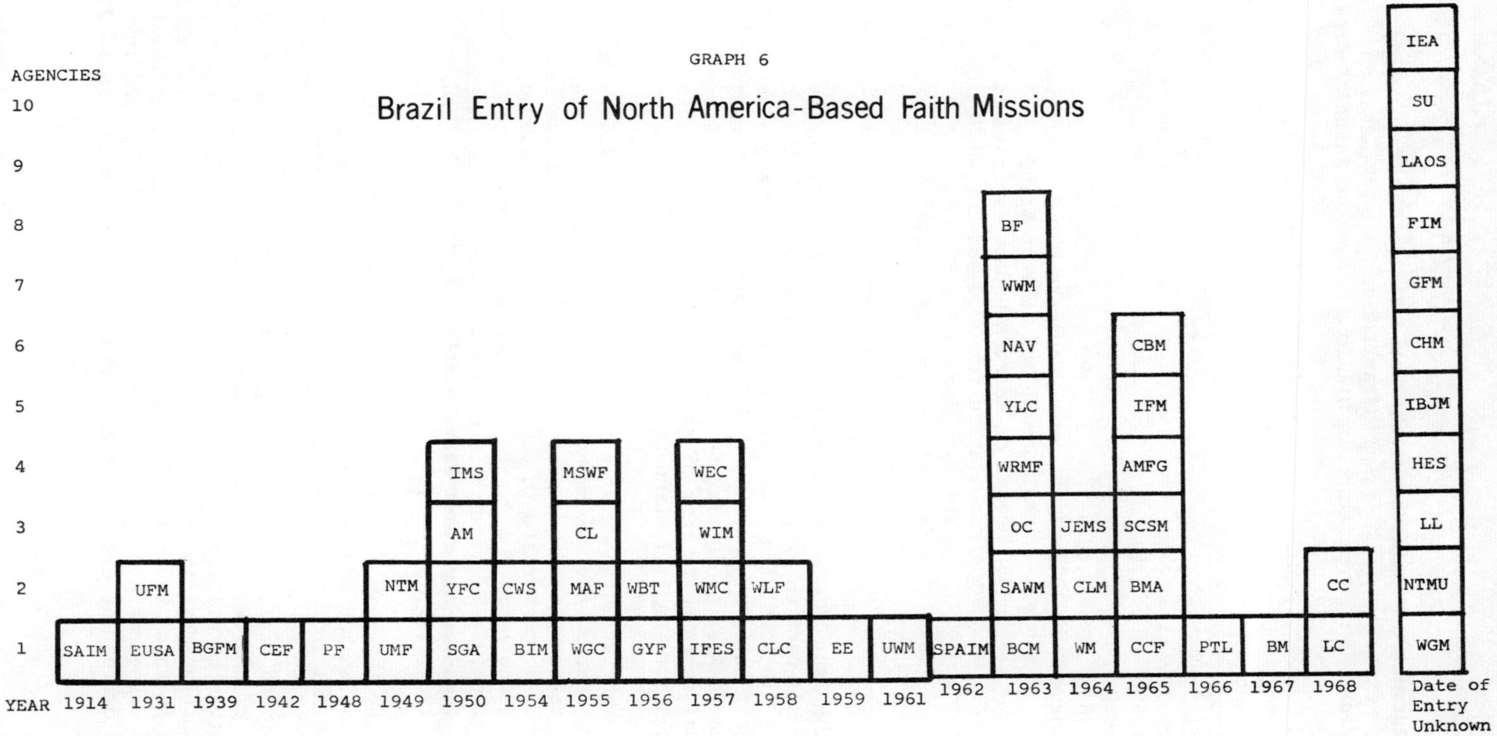

AGENCIES (vertical axis, stacked bottom-to-top by year of entry):

YEAR	Agencies (listed from bottom level 1 upward)
1914	SAIM
1931	EUSA, UFM
1939	BGFM
1942	CEF
1948	PF
1949	UMF, NTM
1950	SGA, YFC, AM, IMS
1954	BIM, CWS
1955	WGC, MAF, CL, MSWF
1956	GYF, WBT
1957	IFES, WMC, WIM, WEC
1958	CLC, WLF
1959	EE
1961	UWM
1962	SPAIM
1963	BCM, SAWM, OC, WRMF, YLC, NAV, WWM, BF
1964	WM, CLM, JEMS, SCSM
1965	CCF, BMA, AMFG, IFM, CBM
1966	PTL
1967	BM
1968	LC, CC

Date of Entry Unknown (stacked column, far right):
WGM, NTMU, LL, HES, IBJM, CHM, GFM, FIM, LAOS, SU, IEA

See List of Abbreviations

Estimated Population of the World Since 1650 Compared to
Brazil

Year	Population in Millions		Average Annual Increase Per 1000 Since Preceding	
	World	Brazil	Date - World	Brazil
1650	524	---	-	-
1750	728	---	3	-
1800	906	---	4	-
1850	1,171	---	5	-
1900	1,608	---	6	-
1950	2,517	---	9	-
1958	2,903	---	18	-
1964	3,220	80	17	31

Source 1650-1900   A. M. Corr. Saunders *World Population: Past Growth and Present Trends*

　　　　1900-1950   based on Corr. Saunders estimate of population for 1900 and United Nations estimate for 1958

　　　　1964   *Statistical Yearbook 1965* p.24   New York: United Nations 1966

(Table indebted to Herr 1968:3).

In the last 300 years the rate of population growth the world over has been unprecedented in human history. This recent increase in population has not been uniformly great; however, the highest rates of increase have been found in the tropical parts of Latin America (Herr 1968:2,3). (Compare Brazil average annual increase to that of the world in the above table).
According to T. Lynn Smith,

Many striking superlatives are being used nowadays to describe the phenomenal increase of population that is taking place throughout the world; but their use is more appropriate in connection with the changes now going on in the twenty American Nations which collectively make up what is commonly known as Latin America than for any other large portion of the earth (Freedman 1964:178).

By the turn of the century it appears that the world's population had mounted to 1,608 millions, of whom some forty-three millions or 2.7 per cent were Latin Americans.
After the close of the first World War the earth's inhabitants had increased to about 1,811 millions whereas the population of the twenty Latin American countries had swollen to about eighty-nine millions or 4.9 per cent of the total. Since 1920 the Latin American countries make up that great world sub-division in which the rate of population increase is the greatest. This was especially pronounced between 1950 and 1960 and remains true during the present decade (Freedman 1964:189). "In 1900

only one out of every thirty-seven members of the human race was
a Latin American, whereas in 1960 the rate had risen to one in
fifteen" (Freedman 1964:179).

The great demographic revolution which began in 1920
throughout Latin America was possibly due in large measure to
the comprehensive health programs of the Rockefeller Foundation
and the world health agencies working in close co-operation with
the governments. The result was a sharp and substantial drop in
the death rate without a corresponding drop in the birth rate.
Except for the tendency for the rate of reproduction to fall in
some sections of the rapidly increasing urban population, the
fertility rates throughout Latin America in general have maintained their previous very high levels (Freedman 1964:182). T.
Lynn Smith predicts that the Latin American population tidal
wave will crest in 1970 at a rate of 3.5 per cent per year because upper and middle class urbanites are beginning to practice
birth control. Some writers predict that by 1980 a sharp reduc-
tion in the birth rate will take place (Freedman 1964:182).

The average world population increase (of 17 per thousand
from 1958-1964) has not been uniformly great. In Latin America
and Africa the population growth is greater than the world average, and at the same time Europe, the United States, Japan and
the U.S.S.R. experienced growth rates somewhat or substantially
lower than the world average (Herr 1968:3).

Brazil with around eighty million persons in 1964 was growing at a rate of thirty-one persons per thousand per year during
the preceding six years. The estimated Brazilian population for
1968 is 90,392,000. Only Mexico (with a growth rate of thirty-
two per thousand) and Costa Rica (which reliably reported a
growth rate of forty-three per thousand) of all the nations of
the world were growing faster than Brazil during the period from
1958 to 1964 (Herr 1968:3).

Thus it is among one of the world's fastest growing populations that the various North American faith missions have been
working during their relatively short Brazilian history.

Redistribution of Population.

Rivaling in importance the spectacular rates at which
the populations of the Latin American countries are
growing are the drastic changes now under way in their
spacial distribution (Freedman 1964:182,183).

Extensive areas of Brazil are entirely devoid of inhabitants
while others are only very sparsely populated. The push of the
settlement of virgin territory is involved to a very limited
extent in the drastic changes in the distribution of population
now under way in Brazil. The tendency of overwhelming importance is the extreme concentration of population growth in the
already densely populated urban centers. Most of the population

increase is accounted for by the mushrooming of existing cities
and by the rapidly mounting numbers of peoples in extensive sub-
urbs, or "bands of misery" which surround the principal urban
centers. This tendency for the population not to push out into
the unsettled portions of the country has left fully half of the
Brazilian land area almost totally unoccupied (see Plate 3).

T. Lynn Smith claims a detailed comparison of the 1950 and
1960 censuses indicates that the only portions of the great Brazilian land mass in which in recent years there has been any
substantial effort to bring new areas into agricultural produc-
tivity are the following: the northwest part of the state of
Parana, the north central portion of the state of Maranhao,
those sections of the state of Goias which are fairly close to
the new national capital (Brasilia), the northern part of the
state of Minas Gerais, and the extreme northwestern part of the
state of Sao Paulo (Freedman 1964:184).

Thanks to the sociological forces at work among dislocated
people, together with the larger economic opportunity which is
available to the uprooted migrant person, these five frontier
areas of Brazil represent the church planter's paradise. Here
are to be found the most receptive Brazilians--Brazilians who
are experiencing change and deliberately making adjustments to
their new situation. This openness to change and readiness to
become innovators is the fertile ground upon which the evangelist can and must sow the seeds of the Gospel with the assured
result of a harvest of new Evangelicals who in turn, with adequate shepherding, can form strong self-propagating local
churches.

Growing Urban Centers. The present rates of population
growth in the urban areas greatly exceed those in rural areas.
The entire process is being fed by the rate of increase of the
total population of at least 3 per cent per year (Freedman 1964:
185). Here is the data: in 1950 about nineteen millions, or
36.5 per cent of the Brazilian population was classified as
urban. During the ensuing ten years Brazil's urban population
increased by more than thirteen millions, or 70 per cent, whereas the rural segment which totaled almost 33.5 millions in 1950
increased merely 5.8 million or by 18 per cent. In this decade
69 per cent of the total increase in Brazil's population took
place in her cities and towns. The most publicized of these was
the immense concentration of people in the cities of Rio de
Janeiro and Sao Paulo. But the rush of Brazilians to the cities
was by no means confined to these two huge giants. Between 1950
and 1960, for example, the urban population of the state of
Minas Gerais increased by more than 1.6 million and that of Rio
Grande do Sul by well over 1,023,000. Indeed, on the relative
basis, the burgeoning of such cities as Belo Horizonte (with
about 700,000 inhabitants in 1960) and Fortaleza (with over
500,000 residents in 1960) was even more spectacular than the

PLATE 3

Population Distribution in Brazil

Ten Largest Cities	Population
1. Rio de Janeiro	3,223,403
2. Sao Paulo	3,164,804
3. Recife	788,569
4. Belo Horizonte	642,912
5. Salvador	630,878
6. Porto Alegre	617,629
7. Belem	349,988
8. Fortaleza	354,942
9. Curitiba	344,560
10. Santos	262,196
(1960 Census)	

I Represents 1/3 of Area
of Brazil
Represents 13/14ths of
Population in Brazil

II Represents 2/3 of Area
of Brazil
Represents 1/14th of
Population in Brazil

Source: Read 1965:124-5, 127

growth of Sao Paulo and Rio de Janeiro. Moreover, Recife and
Salvador both developed so rapidly that they will probably pass
the one million mark before 1970 (Freedman 1964:185,186).

Internal Migration. William Read in his book, *New Patterns
of Church Growth in Brazil,* describes the paths of migrant people within Brazil as five migrational movements:
1) to Brasilia from all directions,
2) to Sao Paulo, Rio de Janeiro and Belo Horizonte in
   South Brazil from the Northeast,
3) from the city of Sao Paulo to Parana, Curitiba, west
   Santa Catarina and to west Rio Grande do Sul in the
   deep South of Brazil,
4) to the west from the city of Sao Paulo into North
   Parana, to all the state of Sao Paulo, to south
   Mato Grosso and
5) rural to urban movement to all large cities (see
   Plate 4).
A good number of the people pushed south by the periodic
droughts are reluctant migrants for their hearts are still in
the Northeast. If these *nordestinos* (Northeasterners) can save
a little money and if the rains return to the Northeast, they
will soon head back home. Thus the traffic on the migratory
paths is to some degree a two-way traffic.

Read indicates that in 1950 the Federal District, Parana,
and Sao Paulo were the top three receivers of the internal migration while Minas Gerais, Bahia, Rio Grande do Sul, Ceara,
Paraiba, Alagoas, Rio de Janeiro and Pernambuco showed the
greatest loss due to these internal migrations (1965:220).

Frontier Minimal Prosperity Means Church Growth Potential.
By contrasting the Arid *Sertao* of the Northeast of Brazil and
the industrial complex which is Sao Paulo to the new coffee boom
area in the northwest of the state of Parana, one gains some
interesting insights into the impact of minimal prosperity on
Evangelical church growth.

Barnett says, "The overall effect of a crisis situation is
restrictive" (1953:12). The personal freedom to explore and to
experience can be constrained by anxieties. People occupied
with subsistence living and devoid of the leisure that is essential to the unhampered manipulation of ideas are not prone to
the acceptance of a novelty.

The poverty areas of northeastern Brazil do indeed show
that both cultural inertia and natural conditions militate
against the freedom to speculate which is of so high a value in
the innovative process. Here people still live in a feudal society carried over from a previous century. Subsistence living
for them is aggravated by periodic droughts. Such conditions
tend to create a mentality resistant to cultural change. It is
primarily as the *nordestino* is pushed south along the migratory

PLATE 4

Migrations in Brazil

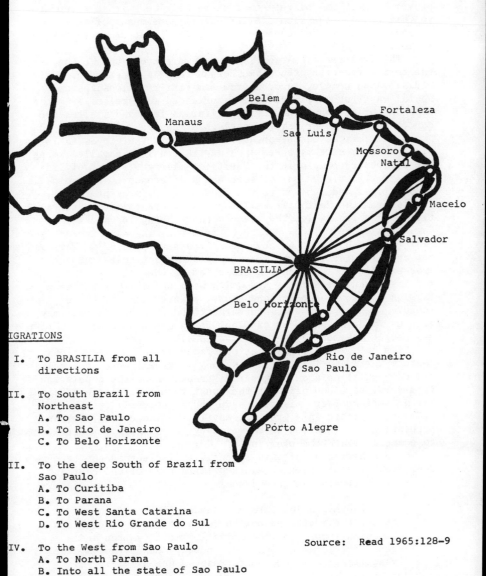

Belem

Manaus

Sao Luis

Fortaleza

Mossoro
Natal

Maceio

Salvador

BRASILIA

Belo Horizonte

Rio de Janeiro
Sao Paulo

Porto Alegre

IGRATIONS

I.   To BRASILIA from all
     directions

II. To South Brazil from
     Northeast
     A. To Sao Paulo
     B. To Rio de Janeiro
     C. To Belo Horizonte

III. To the deep South of Brazil from
     Sao Paulo
     A. To Curitiba
     B. To Parana
     C. To West Santa Catarina
     D. To West Rio Grande do Sul

IV. To the West from Sao Paulo   Source: Read 1965:128-9
     A. To North Parana
     B. Into all the state of Sao Paulo
     C. To South Mato Grosso

V.   To all the large cities (Rural to Urban movements)

routes that he becomes receptive to change. But because the
average migrant is not prepared for the business and industrial
world that is Sao Paulo, his economic condition does not im-
prove. And it is unlikely that there will be a great movement
to Christ among the slum dwellers until some means of incorpo-
rating them into the economic life of the great urban centers
is found.

The frontier situation is largely different and we can take
the coffee frontier of northwestern Parana as an example. Here
a dislocated people, removed from familiar relationships and
social institutions, have also experienced some relief from the
tensions of personal insecurity as far as food and shelter are
concerned. Moreover, they are given a measure of leisure.
Acceptance of the Gospel and of the Protestant ethic is taking
place in such circumstances in a way that has no parallel among
the dislocated people in the "belts of misery" (slums) of Brazil's great cities. Unless some means of economic self-help
is developed and applied to the slum dweller, many of the migrants from the Northeast will shortly return to the conservative region from which they came without being reached for
Christ in either place. "Freedom from pressing want is essential to an exuberance of new ideas" (Barnett 1953:82). This is
not an absolute; in fact, some indigenous Pentecostal groups
have experienced good church growth among the slum dwellers, but
for most Evangelicals the key which will unlock the Brazilian
favelas to the evangelist and church planter remains to be
found. When it is found, and Barnett and the Pentecostals may
help us find this key, we can look for a great turning to Christ
--a people movement among the *favelados*.

The major demographic factors faced by the mid-twentieth
century North American faith missions in Brazil were an accelerated population growth, the redistribution of the population
from rural to urban all over the country and frontier expansion.
North American faith missions have sought to carry out their
missionary effort in a growing, mobile and increasingly urban
population--a situation which we must view as highly receptive
to evangelism and the planting of churches.

A demonstration of this receptivity is seen in the tremendous growth experienced by all Brazilian Evangelical churches to
date. This growth has gone hand in hand with

> . . . the migration into new lands, the building of
> cities, the advancing coffee booms, and the development
> of modern industrial complexes, especially iron and
> steel. National growth has, indeed, opened the way for
> evangelization (Read, Monterroso, Johnson 1969:42).

Having reconstructed the Brazilian regional and demographic
context of the North American faith missions, we turn to examine
the nature of their field activity. To what extent has their
strategy taken into account the factors we have surveyed in this
chapter?

4

The Field Activity

of the Faith Missions

THE FIVE TYPES OF NORTH AMERICAN FAITH MISSIONS WITH NO DIRECT
INVOLVEMENT IN CHURCH PLANTING

In 1969 thirty-one agencies with 108 missionaries in Brazil
were involved in specialized ministries which can be classified
broadly into five types: the non-sending funding agency, the
forwarding agency, the agency which specializes in child or
youth evangelism, the agency specializing in ethnic group evangelism and the service agency. This means that fully 50 per
cent of the faith mission agencies with 13 per cent of the faith
missionary force are not directly involved in a church planting
ministry and have no goal of developing a church or denomination
in Brazil.

The Non-sending Funding Agency. Not all the horizontal
support base mission agencies have missionary personnel in Brazil. Of four such agencies the best known is World Vision International. Its emphasis is on the support of orphans, pastors'
conferences, the funding of special projects and most recently
the MARC program of mission research in co-operation with the
Brazil Missionary Information Bureau (MIB). The other three
agencies provide Christian literature in the Portuguese language: Gospel Literature in National Tongues, World Literature
Crusade and Bible Literature International.

The Forwarding Agency. The Pilgrim Fellowship, Inc. would
claim no work in Brazil but views its task as handling funds for
independent faith missionaries. There are four independent
faith missionaries currently in Brazil being served by PF. A
similar agency is the Fellowship of Independent Missions which
serves two independent faith missionaries in Brazil, one of whom
is designated a church planter.

The Agency Which Specializes in Child or Youth Evangelism.
Seven faith mission agencies with thirty-four missionaries focus
their attention, efforts and energies to reach children and
youth through college age.

The Child Evangelism Fellowship which entered Brazil in
1942 has ten missionaries actively engaged in reaching Brazilian
children with the message of salvation. This mission has provided a fine body of literature mostly translated from its English language materials for the purpose of evangelizing Brazilian children.

Youth for Christ, Word of Life and Young Life Campaign entered Brazil in 1950, 1958 and 1963, respectively, and focus
their effort largely on those of high school age. Each differs
somewhat as to its methods and approach but all seem to have
followed the lead of Word of Life in using camping to reach
teens for Christ. Word of Life also has a Bible school in Sao
Paulo to train Christian workers.

Three other agencies which specialize in sub-culture evangelism aim primarily at the college-age youth of Brazil. The
earliest to send missionaries to Brazil was the International
Fellowship of Evangelical Students (1957). The IFES has no work
of its own in Brazil but loans two missionaries to the fully
autonomous Alianca Biblica Universitaria do Brasil (ABUB). In
1963 the Navigators of Colorado Springs, Colorado, entered the
Brazil field and have worked at their university center in Curitiba, Parana, in a program of evangelism and leadership training. They were followed in 1968 by the California-based Campus
Crusade for Christ.

There is obviously a great need for student and youth work
but it appears that there is even a greater need for missionaries working under the auspices of these agencies that specialize
in youth and student evangelism to see to it that converts find
their way quickly into local churches. It is apparent that a
general suspicion of the denominations pervades the thinking of
many of these missionaries as well as their colleagues in other
faith missions. A North American missionary serving with one
such a group was asked when he was going to direct a year-old
convert into a local church. He replied, "I don't know any
church in which I have confidence." There is a large place in
Brazil for student and youth evangelism but it needs to be related to local churches. This "cultural overhang" of the faith
or interdenominational missionary must be overcome. He must
relate to the spiritually vital and growing Brazilian Evangelical Church in a more dynamic way. As these missionaries have
been praiseworthy leaders in youth evangelism and leadership
training, they should now also become trail blazers in relating
their knowledge, experience and gifts to the on-going life of
the visible body of Christ in Brazil--the local churches.

The Agency Specializing in Ethnic Group Evangelism. Eight North American Protestant missionaries representing four faith mission agencies are working among two ethnic communities: the Japanese and Jewish people. One missionary serving under the auspices of the Japanese Evangelical Mission Society is working with Japanese immigrants. The other seven missionaries serving with the Hebrew Evangelization Society, The International Board of Jewish Missions and The Cleveland Hebrew Mission are involved in the evangelization of Jews. None of these agencies have as their objective the establishing a church or a denomination.

The So-called Service Agency. By far the largest group of faith missionaries not directly involved in planting churches (fifteen agencies with sixty-two persons) fall into this classification. These define their mission as service. The writer recently attended a conference of the largest mission agency in this group--The Overseas Crusades (thirteen missionaries in Brazil)--where the ideal of helping the "whole body of Christ" to evangelize was prevalent throughout. It is also noteworthy that OC has been one of the first of the faith missions to come to an appreciation of the "church growth" perspective. OC implements its enthusiasm by publishing bi-monthly the *Church Growth Bulletin* edited by Dr. Donald McGavran and sending its field directors to the Fuller School of World Mission-Institute of Church Growth in Pasadena, California. The basic program of Overseas Crusades as described in the *Handbook of Principles and Policies* is threefold:
    A.   Training the Church in evangelism. This includes
         pastors' conferences and training institutes to
         motivate and train believers as active witnesses.
    B.   Mobilizing the Church for evangelism in individual
         churches or united in gospel crusades.
    C.   Edifying the Church by means of:
         1.   Bible correspondence courses, short-term Bible
              training institutes.
         2.   Bible conferences in local churches (1968:3).
Therefore service as conceptualized by OC is helping mission-related and indigenous churches to evangelize and thereby to grow.

The services rendered by other agencies of this classification range from relief and orphanage work, such as that done by the Church World Service and the Christian Children's Fund, to transportation, such as that provided by the Missionary Aviation Fellowship. Two other organizations are involved in radio work (World Radio Missionary Fellowship and World Gospel Crusades); but by far the largest number of the service agencies are involved in efforts which are connected with literature and literacy. The Southern Cross Scripture Mission is concerned solely with the distribution of the Scriptures in the Portuguese language, while the Bible Memory Association is encouraging the memorization of the Scriptures. Laubach Literacy, Inc., like its great

founder and namesake, is committed to the task of lowering Bra-
zil's illiteracy rate (nearly 50 per cent). The Christian Life
Mission publishes O Mundo Cristao, the colorful, attractive and
Brazil-oriented Portuguese counterpart of the English language
Christian Life magazine. Other agencies such as the Pocket
Testament League, Christian Literature Crusade and World Gospel
Crusade link the provision of literature to active direct evangelism. Still others such as Go-Ye Fellowship are finding mean-
ingful service in diverse and unique ways. One such notable way
is the ministry of GYF's Frank Ineson as director of the Brazil-
based Missionary Information Bureau.

THE COMPARATIVE SIZE OF THE NORTH AMERICAN BASED FAITH MISSIONS

The average size of the North American faith mission agency
at work in Brazil measured by its field personnel is 13.7 missionaries. The one closest to this average size is one which
has fourteen missionaries. In addition to noting the average
size, the faith missions can be brought into sharper focus by
classifying them according to size in three groups as may be
seen in Graph 7:
     1) agencies with one to five missionaries,
     2) agencies with between six and fourteen missionaries
     3) and the nine largest North American faith agencies.
Of the sixty-one faith missions at work in Brazil thirty-
nine have between one and five missionaries each. Thus we see
that over half, or to be exact, 63.9 per cent of these agencies
account for less than 10 per cent of the North American faith
missionary force. Another fourteen agencies with between six
and fourteen missionaries each comprise 16.2 per cent (136 missionaries) of the North American faith missionary force. But a
full 75 per cent of the faith missionary force serve with only
nine of the sixty-one agencies. Moreover, of these nine agencies three alone have an aggregate of 447 missionaries and comprise 53.7 per cent of the total North American faith missionary
force. These three are the Wycliffe Bible Translators with 173
missionaries, Unevangelized Fields Mission with 140 and New
Tribes Mission with 134. Each of the three is involved in a
church planting ministry. (Wycliffe plants churches and turns
them over to other agencies for care.)
Since together these three largest faith missions account
for so large a part of the total faith missionary force, it is
important to know where and among what segment of the population
they are conducting their missionary effort. All are involved,
two exclusively, in tribal work in the Eastern Highlands, the
Northeastern Coast, and Amazon Lowlands and the South. Wycliffe
has workers concentrating on twenty-six Brazilian Indian tribes
(Goddard 1967:713). The New Tribes Mission specializes in evangelizing and planting the indigenous church among still other

GRAPH 7

COMPARATIVE SIZE OF FAITH MISSIONS BY PERSONNEL

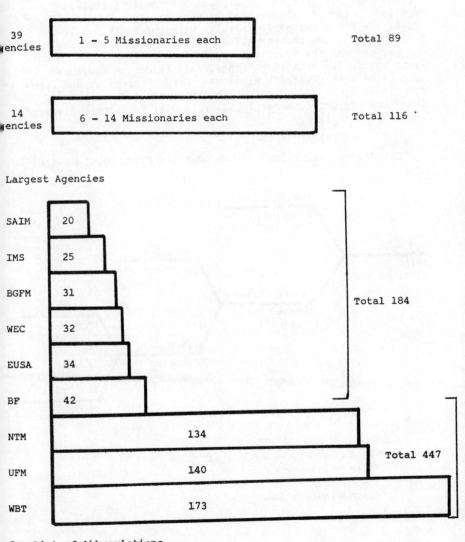

39
agencies   1 - 5 Missionaries each   Total 89

14
agencies   6 - 14 Missionaries each   Total 116

Largest Agencies

SAIM   20
IMS   25
BGFM   31
WEC   32   Total 184
EUSA   34
BF   42
NTM   134
UFM   140   Total 447
WBT   173

See List of Abbreviations
Source: Research questionnaire by author

unreached Indians (Correspondence, Hare, 1969). The UFM had in
mid 1966, 15 per cent of its missionary force deployed in tribal
work. Assuming this distribution to be constant for 1969, twenty-one UFM missionaries would be currently working among Brazil's tribal people.

While Indians in South America are 8.5 per cent of the total population, the Amerindians in Brazil make up far less than
one per cent of the total population (Horton 1966:10,11,13).
Here is a situation illuminated in part by Graph 7. It shows
175 of the 927 missionaries serving with the North American
faith missions are concentrating their efforts on far less than
one per cent of the Brazilian population. This helps us understand why so few Brazilian Evangelicals belong to churches
associated with the faith missions. Read, Monterroso and Johnson (1969:66,67) indicate that this percentage is only one-
fourth of one per cent for 1965. This will be further discussed
in the next section.

STATISTICAL ANALYSIS OF NORTH AMERICAN FAITH MISSIONARIES

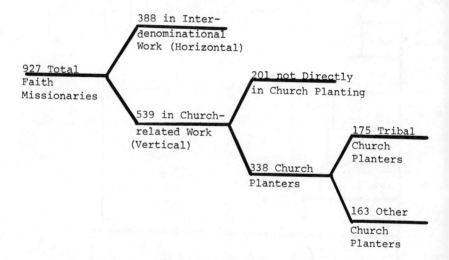

Note: 163 is only 17.6% of the 927
        faith missionaries and even
        338 is only 36.5% of the 927
        faith missionaries.

WHO ARE THE CHURCH PLANTERS AMONG THE FAITH MISSIONS?

A superficial evaluation based on a previous section might leave one with the impression that the bulk of the North American faith mission force in Brazil is involved in planting Evangelical churches among some of the most receptive people in the world. Such, as we will see, is not the case. True enough, twenty-nine agencies or approximately 48 per cent of the North American faith mission agencies have some commitment to plant churches.* But an actual count, as seen in the diagram above, of the number of missionaries (not agencies) declared church planters by their agencies is 338, which is more than half of the 539 who are in vertical work. Of these 338, ninety, fifty and twenty-one respectively are indicated as working "among the tribes" by the three largest North American faith agencies, NTM, WBT, and UFM. To these must be added the South American Indian Mission with fourteen declared church planters among the Indians making a total of 175 in a somewhat ambiguous category. These facts change our understanding of the faith missions as church planters in two notable ways. First, we do not know how many "among the tribes" are actually involved in church planting or what part of the time and effort of those who are planting churches is taken up in translation, literacy and other works perhaps not directly involved in the church planting task. We merely know in general that such efforts are often dynamically linked to the establishing of churches among tribal people. Secondly, there is the fact already noted that the above 175 missionaries (out of 338 declared church planters) are involved with far less than one per cent of the Brazilian population. The remaining 163 declared church planters (a mere 17.6 per cent of the total North American faith missionary force) are laboring among the millions of Brazilians in the larger, receptive sectors of the population. We are forced to conclude at this point in our study that a 17.6 per cent personnel involvement in the church planting task among receptive Brazilians, in light of the unprecedented opportunity afforded Evangelicals in Brazil, is meager indeed.

Furthermore, it is not enough to know that 163 church planters associated with North American faith missions are working among the receptive "neo-Brazilians". We must now ask where these church planters are located in the regional complexity of Brazil, which we have described in Chapter 3.

*The one unaccounted for mission, the Amazon Mission, has indicated in a letter to the writer that it is disbanding its pioneer work in the Amazon Lowlands. As of April, 1969, it retained only a daily radio broadcast.

THE REGIONAL DISTRIBUTION OF THE CHURCH-PLANTING FAITH AGENCIES

We focus our attention now on the twenty-nine North American faith mission agencies which have the declared purpose of planting churches. We will observe the particular region or regions in which these agencies are at work as they make their contribution to the growth of the Evangelical Church. The developed South has the largest concentration (nineteen) of church-planting faith missions. Five others are located in Brazil's Eastern Highlands and five more are working in the Amazon Lowlands. Three church-planting faith missions are located in each of the three remaining regions--the Far West, the Northeast Coast and the Northeast Arid *Sertao* (see Plate 5).

The South. Twelve of nineteen agencies, which have thirty-five declared church planters, work solely in the South. Four others have work in the South and in one other Brazilian region. The remaining three have work in two other regions.

List of Church-Planting Faith Missions Working Solely in the South

Agency	Number of Declared Missionary Church Planters
Spanish American Inland Mission	4
West Indies Mission	5
United World Mission	3
Missionary Soul Winning Fellowship	6
Slavic Gospel Association	5
Evangelical Enterprises	4
Co-Laborers	0
Bible Conference and Missions	2
Fellowship of Independent Missionaries	1
United Missionary Fellowship	3
World Gospel Mission	Co-operate with denomination
Inter-American Missionary Society	2

The Worldwide Evangelization Crusade (H - V94%, H6%) divides its missionary force of thirty-two persons between Sao Paulo (two) and Minas Gerais (thirty). Twenty-six missionaries are declared church planters. This means that no less than twenty-four WEC church-planting missionaries are concentrating on the Eastern Highlands.

The Bethany Fellowship (H - H91%, V9%) has forty-two missionaries, four of whom are church planters. BF divides its effort between the South (northwestern Parana where it began its work in 1963) and the Eastern Highlands (central Minas Gerais).

An MIB questionnaire in 1965 indicated that at that time

World Wide Missions (H - V50%, H50%) had no missionaries in Brazil. A response to the author's questionnaire in 1969, however, reports that two missionaries have since entered the country, one minister and one layman. WWM identifies one as a church planter. It works in Ubatuba, Sao Paulo, in the South and in Guanabara and the state of Rio de Janeiro in the Eastern Highlands.

The Brazil Inland Mission (H - V100%) has eight missionaries who are church planters and headquartered at Umuramã in the northwestern Parana. BIM also has missionary personnel in the state of Mato Grosso in the Brazilian Far West.

Three of the church planting faith missions located in the South have missionaries in two other Brazilian regions. These three, listed in order of the size of their missionary force, are New Tribes Mission, New Testament Missionary Union and United Missionary Fellowship. The New Tribes Mission (H - V100%) working in the Amazon Lowlands has part of its missionary force deployed in the Eastern Highlands as well as in the South. The NTM majors in evangelism and church planting among tribal people. The New Testament Missionary Union has ten ministers engaged in planting and establishing churches "that are independent of foreign direction" (Correspondence, 1969). Missionaries establish but do not pastor the churches (Goddard 1967:953). The United Missionary Fellowship (formerly the Pioneer Bible Mission) establishes local, independent fundamental churches. It also maintains a youth camp and a Bible Institute.

The Eastern Highlands. Five missions are dedicated to planting churches in the Eastern Highlands. This region includes almost the entirety of the states of Minas Gerais and Rio de Janeiro, all but the coastal region of the state of Bahia and the eastern part of the state of Goias where the new national capital, Brasilia, has been built.

We have already spoken of four missions which work in the South as well as here in the Eastern Highlands: the Worldwide Evangelization Crusade, World Wide Missions, Bethany Fellowship and New Tribes Mission.

Unevangelized Fields Mission (H - V97%, H3%) has its sixty church planters in three Brazilian regions--Eastern Highlands, Amazon Lowlands and the Northeast Arid *Sertao*. Of the sixty, twenty-one are assigned to tribal work.

The Amazon Lowlands. Five faith missions have church-planting missionaries deployed in this region. Three of these we have already treated with the other regions (NTM, UMF, NTMU).

The Evangelical Union of South America, one of the agencies that has shifted its home base from England to the United States (Lindsell 1962:203), has eighteen North American missionaries deployed as church planters in the Amazon Lowlands, the Northeast Arid *Sertao* and the Northeast Coast.

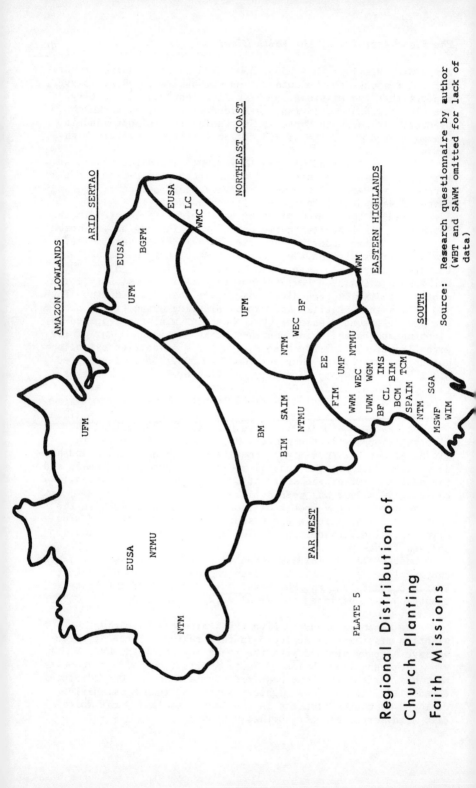

PLATE 5

Regional Distribution of
Church Planting
Faith Missions

AMAZON LOWLANDS

ARID SERTAO

NORTHEAST COAST

EASTERN HIGHLANDS

SOUTH

FAR WEST

Source: Research questionnaire by author
(WBT and SAWM omitted for lack of
data)

The Far West. We have already treated the New Testament Missionary Union and the Brazil Inland Mission under other regions; two other church-planting faith agencies work in the Far West. The South American Indian Mission (H - V100%), as the name of the mission states, is concerned with tribal work and has fourteen church planters in the state of Mato Grosso. Berean Mission which entered the country in 1967 has its lone missionary couple deployed as church planters in Mato Grosso.

The Northeast Arid Sertao. Brazil Gospel Fellowship Mission (H - V89%, H11%) concentrates its missionary effort in the state of Ceara. BGFM entered Brazil in 1939 and presently has twenty-seven missionaries designated as church planters.
The Evangelical Union of South America and Unevangelized Fields Mission (previously treated under other regions) are the only other North American based church-planting faith missions in this Brazilian region which, besides the state of Ceara, includes portions of Maranhao, Piaui, Pernambuco, Paraiba, and Rio Grande do Norte.

The Northeast Coast. Three faith missions have church planters deployed on the Northeast Coast which includes the states of Alagoas, Sergipe and Espirito Santo and portions of Bahia, Pernambuco, Paraiba and Rio Grande do Norte. The Evangelical Union of South America has been previously treated.
Literature Crusades (H - V100%) entered Brazil in 1968 and reports that it has its full missionary force, five designated church planters, in Recife. LC's "work includes gospel outreach, literature distribution, and correspondence course" (Correspondence, 1969).
World Missions to Children (H - V88%, H12%) has been in Brazil twelve years and currently has one-half of its missionary force (four) deployed as church planters in Pernambuco where the mission also has a clinic, school and orphanage.

PROFILES OF SIX CHURCH-PLANTING NORTH AMERICAN FAITH MISSIONS

Five of the following agencies are chosen from among those North American faith missions involved in the church-planting task in Brazil for two principal reasons. The first reason is a desire to have agencies representative of the whole spectrum of the Brazilian history of the North American faith missions. The second reason was dictated by the available church growth statistics. A sixth agency, the Inter-American Missionary Society, is included because it is the subject of our study of a successful church-planting faith mission in Chapter 5.

The South American Indian Mission. The Florida-based South American Indian Mission (H - V100%) with a fifty-six year history is the oldest North American faith mission in Brazil. SAIM

was in the country pioneering tribal work seventeen years before
the entrance of any other existing faith mission from North America.
     The stated purpose of the SAIM is to go to the unreached
Indians in interior South America to preach, establish self-
supporting, self-propagating and self-governing native churches
(Goddard 1967:1222).   In 1969 of the twenty SAIM missionaries,
fourteen were deployed in the church planting task.
     As indicated in Graph 8 the SAIM in 1957 after forty-three
years of Brazilian endeavor had 450 communicants in its national
church. This was an average annual addition of about ten communicants. No doubt this small beginning can be accounted for
in part by the governmental restriction placed on Indian work in
the 1930's. This restriction continued through most of the
1940's. None the less this is hardly perceptible church growth.
     We do not know the pattern of SAIM growth prior to 1957.
Graph 9 assumes the work began with ten communicant members in
1914. Even with this assumption the growth following 1957 as a
percentage increase is not spectacular. There are three stages
indicated by the graph. During the years 1957-1962 the church
was experiencing a 2.1 per cent growth rate per year. By 1960
there were ten SAIM churches and five unorganized regular meeting places in the state of Mato Grosso where the mission also
maintained sixteen institutions. In the second stage (1963-
1965) SAIM churches saw an increased annual growth rate of 6.3.
In the next two years the growth rate increased to 8.6 per cent
per year. A projection made on the basis of the 1966-1967
growth rate indicates that there were approximately 700 communicant members in the national church related to SAIM in 1968.
     By reference to Table 2 and Graph 9 we note that after
fifty-four years the communicant members produced by SAIM make
up two of every ten thousand Evangelical communicants in Brazil
and is growing at less than the national average of eleven per
cent per year. Concentration of effort on a small resistant
population coupled with the protracted period of government re-
strictions on the tribal work mentioned above are some of the
factors that account for the small church growth experienced by
the churches related to SAIM. One can not help but wonder if
specializing on tribal people to the exclusion of the receptive
sectors of the nation's populace is the best course of action
open to the SAIM when there are great church planting and developing opportunities available in the frontier pockets of the
same Brazilian state where SAIM is conducting its missionary
effort. This is not meant to suggest that evangelism and church
planting among tribal people in Brazil be abandoned. It is
rather meant to suggest that the possibility be studied by SAIM
of diversifing its work with an eye to seizing the great opportunity afforded it by the receptive Brazilians in the Far West
region.

The Unevangelized Fields Mission. In 1931 the UFM (H - V97%, H3%) entered Brazil and is the second oldest and second largest (140 missionaries) existing North American faith mission there. Like the SAIM, Unevangelized Fields Mission at first concentrated on tribal work. "Fourteen tribes were reached" (CGRILA Correspondence, 1966) by the first missionaries. Then suddenly came the government restriction on Indian work. The missionaries rather than returning to the homeland, turned to the civilized Brazilian population. The UFM met the restrictive situation by turning to the more receptive population of the Northeast Coast, the Amazon Lowlands and the Eastern Highlands.

In mid 1966, 16 per cent of the UFM missionary force was deployed in tribal work. If this percentage held constant, it would mean that twenty-one UFM missionaries are currently deployed in tribal work. This interdenominational faith mission has seventeen stations in Brazil and carries on launch evangelism on the Amazon River.

The national church founded by UFM is the Alianca das Igrejas Cristas Evangelicas do Norte do Brasil. In 1949, eighteen years after its Brazil entry, the national church founded by UFM had 1,000 communicant members. This was an average annual increase of fifty-six communicants. The average annual growth rate for 1950, 1951 and 1952 was 14.5 per cent. During the years 1953-1958 the church was growing at the average annual rate of 6.5 per cent. In the next year the Alianca gained 850 communicnat members--a growth rate for 1959 of 27.8 per cent. The Alianca then grew to 5,800 communicants in 1967 nearly doubling its size in eight years (see Graph 8).

At this writing, all but four of the UFM missionary staff are involved in direct church planting ministries. The UFM is an example of a large faith mission that has taken its church-planting opportunity seriously by using a large proportion of its missionaries in the church-planting task, by financial assistance to national pastors and by a working plan of mission-national church relationship whereby churches planted by missionaries are turned over to the Alianca. In the last seventeen years the national church related to the UFM has multiplied itself nearly five times. If the rate of growth of the UFM between 1960 and 1967 is projected to 1968, we arrive at a membership of approximately 6,200 (see Graph 9).

Table 2 shows that after thirty-seven years 17.5 communicant members out of every ten thousand Evangelical communicants in Brazil belong to UFM-sponsored churches. It also shows that these churches are growing at a slightly greater rate (11.3 per cent) than the national annual growth rate.

Brazil Gospel Fellowship Mission. Eight years after the UFM began in Brazil, the fourth extant North American faith mission entered to begin its Brazilian endeavor in 1939. Brazil Gospel Fellowship Mission (H - V87%, H13%) with a missionary

force of thirty-one persons is the seventh largest North America-based faith mission at work in the country. BGFM in its work
of establishing independent, autonomous local churches is located in the state of Ceara within the Northeast Arid *Sertao* region. Twenty-seven BGFM missionaries are involved in work related to the national church and are designated church planters.
In 1969 BGFM had established three self-governing churches. In
two of these churches machinery for self-propagation is completely in the control of the national church. One of the three is
also self-supporting. In addition, the mission has ten stations,
numerous outstations and a short term Bible Institute (Goddard
1967:182).

After twenty-five years of labor (in 1963) the churches related to BGFM had 152 communicant members--an average annual increase of six communicants. In 1964 fifty-one additional communicants were received into the national churches. BGFM
churches grew 33.6 per cent on a base of 152 for this one year.
(No statistics are available for the following years.) (See
Graph 8.)

This Evangelical, interdenominational, conservative, Calvinistic faith mission has made a small contribution to the total number of Evangelical communicants in Brazil. Table 2 and
Graph 9 illuminate several aspects of their growth. By project-
ing the number of communicants in the churches related to BGFM
we find that there were close to 484 in 1967. It can now be
estimated that after twenty-nine years the communicant members
produced by BGFM missionaries constitute 1.2 persons in every
ten thousand Evangelical communicnats in Brazil. The church is
growing at three times the national average rate on a base of
200.

Two factors have probably inhibited the growth of this long
term faith missionary agency. The BGFM has located its work in
the resistant Northeast Arid *Sertao* limiting itself to the state
of Ceara so that despite a fine commitment to the church-planting task (twenty-seven missionaries), little church growth has
resulted.

There is another factor that would bear investigation. The
doctrinal statement of the agency appears to be very important
to the mission, as it is spelled out with detail and clarity as
interdenominational, conservative and Calvinistic. Do we have
here an illustration of the orientation of the faith missionary
described in Chapter 1? Has the concern for doctrinal purity
as understood in North American terms served to inhibit the
growth of the national church? The greatest church growth in-
hibitor may well be the religious-cultural orientation of the
agency and its missionaries rather than the region or the concentration of the missionaries.

Brazil Inland Mission. Headquartered in the frontier city
of Umurama in northwestern Parana, the Brazil Inland Mission

(H - V100%) has been carrying out its three-fold purpose to evangelize, train national workers and establish national self-supporting churches since 1954. This agency reports eight missionaries, all church planters, working mainly in the southern state of Parana. BIM indicates that its work in Mato Grosso is uncertain.

Taylor gives ninety-one as the number of communicant members for the BIM national church in 1960 (1961:40). This would be an average annual increase of thirteen communicants. In a letter to William R. Read, O. R. Bartlett estimates 1200 as the number of communicant members of the church related to BIM in 1967. *If this estimate is accurate,* then the national church of this agency has multiplied itself a full twelve times in seven years (see Graph 8). A projection based on the growth rate indicated by the Bartlett estimate gives approximately 1,450 communicants for 1968.

As may be seen in Table 2 and Graph 9 after fourteen years the communicant members produced by BIM constitute 3.6 communicants in every ten thousand Evangelical communicants in Brazil and the church is growing at nearly ten times (103 per cent) the national average growth rate per year.

Worldwide Evangelization Crusade. 1957 marks the entrance into Brazil of the Worldwide Evangelization Crusade (H - V94%, H6%). As reported above, its thirty-two missionaries are divided between Sao Paulo (two) in the South and Minas Gerais (thirty) within the Eastern Highlands region. Of the thirty-two missionaries, twenty-six are designated church planters while two are devoted to evangelistic conference work and the other two are in field leadership and printing. At least twenty-four of the church planters are located in the state of Minas Gerais. Six of them work in co-operation with an organized conference and twenty are not connected with any organization. When the churches founded by these missionaries

> are adult and can support their own pastor, they may
> choose their denomination or continue as an indepen-
> dent Evangelical church. We as a mission have not
> created a denomination and do not intend to (Cor-
> respondence, WEC 1969).

Communicant members in the churches founded by WEC missionaries grew from twenty in 1957 to thirty-five in 1958, then to fifty-five in 1959 and on to eighty in 1960. In these first four years the churches related to WEC experienced an average annual addition of twenty communicants. In the following four years (1961-1964) the churches experienced an average annual growth rate of 32.6 per cent. An estimated number of communicants for 1967 made on the basis of the 1961-1964 growth rate would be 600.

As may be seen in Table 2 and Graph 9 in eleven years (1957
-1967) WEC missionaries have produced 600 communicant members or
1.6 communicants in every ten thousand Evangelical communicants
in Brazil. Though this proportion is low it must be remembered
that the churches related to WEC are growing at nearly three
times the national rate for Evangelical communicants.

The Inter-American Missionary Society. The Brazil entry
date for IMS (H - H58%, V42%) missionaries was 1950. There are
presently twenty-five IMS missionaries working in the southern
states of Parana and Sao Paulo. Eleven of these missionaries
are involved in work related to the national church and two are
designated church planters.

In the ninth year (1958) of its Brazilian endeavor the
national church related to the IMS had 310 communicant members.
This was a yearly average increase of thirty-four communicants.
In the following nine years (1959-1967) the national church grew
to an estimated 1750 communicant members. In this latter period
the national church multiplied itself nearly six times. A projection of the communicant members in 1968 made on the basis of
the growth rate for 1966 and 1967 would be approximately 2,350
(see Graph 9).

The annual growth rate for the church related to the IMS is
as follows:

                1962 - 1963 ------- 41.8%
                1963 - 1964 ------- 35.5%
                1964 - 1965 ------- 22.3%
                1965 - 1966 ------- 36.3%
                1966 - 1967 ------- 29.6%

After eighteen years the communicant members gained by the IMS
constitute 5.3 communicants out of each ten thousand Evangelical communicants in Brazil and are growing at three times the
national average (see Table 2 and Graph 9).

The IMS of Brazil is the case study that we will treat in
depth in the next chapter.

TABLE 2

COMPARATIVE GROWTH RATES OF CHURCHES RELATED TO SIX CHURCH-PLANTING FAITH MISSIONS

Name of Church-Planting Agency	Date of Entry	Years of Brazilian Effort	Missionaries in Vertical Work	Declared Church-Planting Missionaries	Number of Communicant Members 1967	Number of Communicants Per Ten Thousand Evangelical Communicants	Annual Growth Rate Compared with National Average (N.A. = 11%) for All Evangelical Communicants
South American Indian Mission	1914	54	20	14	650	2	8.6% (=78% of N.A.)
Unevangelized Fields Mission	1931	37	136	60	5,800	17.5	11.3% (=103% of N.A.)
Brazil Gospel Fellowship Mission	1939	29	27	27	484	1.4	33.6% (=305% of N.A.)
Inter-American Missionary Society	1950	18	11	2	1,750	5.3	38% (=345% of N.A.)
Brazil Inland Mission	1954	14	8	8	1,200	3.6	103% (935% of N.A.)
Worldwide Evangelization Crusade	1957	11	30	26	600	1.6	32.6% (=290% of N.A.)

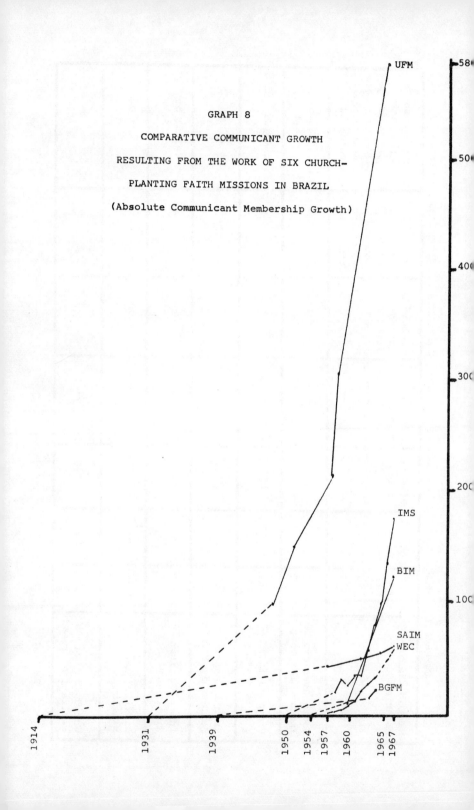

GRAPH 8

COMPARATIVE COMMUNICANT GROWTH

RESULTING FROM THE WORK OF SIX CHURCH-

PLANTING FAITH MISSIONS IN BRAZIL

(Absolute Communicant Membership Growth)

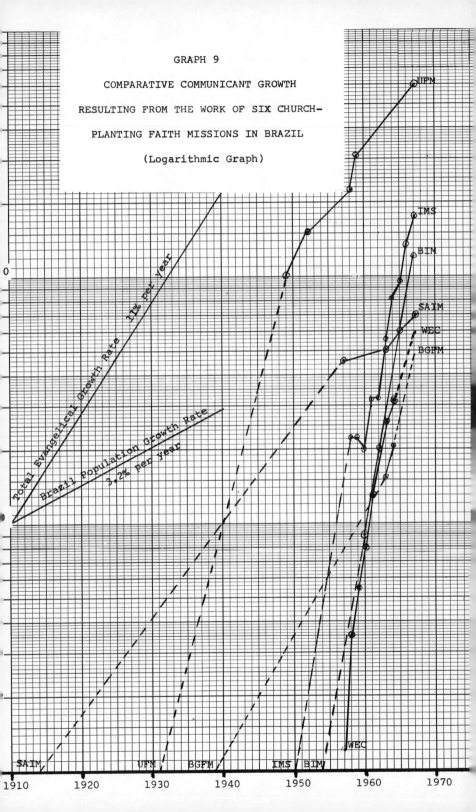

GRAPH 9

COMPARATIVE COMMUNICANT GROWTH

RESULTING FROM THE WORK OF SIX CHURCH-

PLANTING FAITH MISSIONS IN BRAZIL

(Logarithmic Graph)

PLATE 6

TYPOLOGY OF SIX CHURCH—PLANTING FAITH MISSIONS SYMBOLIZED

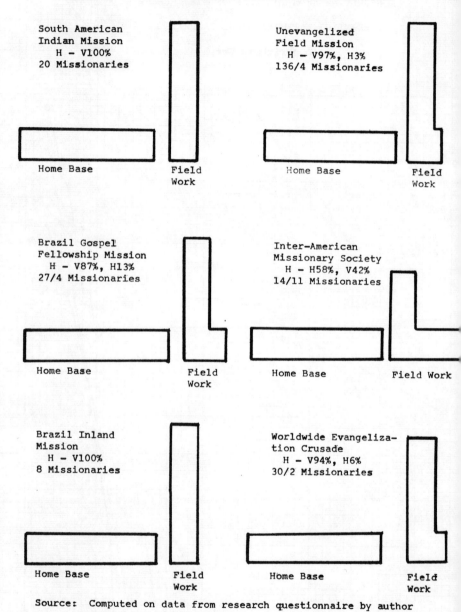

South American
Indian Mission
H — V100%
20 Missionaries

Home Base

Field
Work

Unevangelized
Field Mission
H — V97%, H3%
136/4 Missionaries

Home Base

Field
Work

Brazil Gospel
Fellowship Mission
H — V87%, H13%
27/4 Missionaries

Home Base

Field
Work

Inter—American
Missionary Society
H — H58%, V42%
14/11 Missionaries

Home Base

Field Work

Brazil Inland
Mission
H — V100%
8 Missionaries

Home Base

Field
Work

Worldwide Evangeliza-
tion Crusade
H — V94%, H6%
30/2 Missionaries

Home Base

Field
Work

Source: Computed on data from research questionnaire by author

5

A Successful

Church-Planting Faith Mission

The reason for the good growth of the church related to the Inter-American Missionary Society in Brazil has apparently not been due to the ministry of missionaries for the actual involvement of IMS missionaries in the church-planting task is small. In 1969 this agency said that only two of its staff of twenty-five missionaries are deployed as church planters.

In fact, of the three largest local churches related to the denomination created by the IMS effort, not one was founded through the effort of the IMS missionaries. Two were planted by independent missionaries (Suzano, Sao Paulo, by Rev. Carl Cooper and the Avenida Parana Church of Londrina, Parana, by Rev. Roderick Davies) prior to the Brazil entry of the IMS and were turned over together with other churches to the mission.

The large segment of IMS missionaries is involved not in church-planting but in the church-developing ministry, e.g., ministries more or less complementary to the national church. It is important to note that missionaries in these ministries have managed to maintain their interdenominational orientation (described in Chapter 1) throughout the nineteen years of their Brazilian endeavor. Some ministries have made and/or are making a negligible contribution to the growth of the national church. Two examples are the now discontinued *Revival* magazine and the daily radio broadcast. The values of radio in its present form beyond interdenominational evangelism are its promotional appeal in the sending country and its advertising value for the Bible Institute and Seminary on the field.

The negative effect of this interdenominational emphasis in the Bible School, the radio broadcast and the Crusade, which will be mentioned below, was to convince the leaders, pastors and workers of the national church of the divided interest of the missionaries in regard to its welfare and program. A positive result of the interdenominational preoccupation of the

missionaries was the large degree of autonomy allowed to the
national church by the mission.

Since the growth of the national church depends primarily
on the effort of national workers, good relations between the
mission agency and the national church are clearly of paramount
importance. Therefore, our study will examine the field work
and orientation of the IMS missionaries and the relations that
have developed between themselves and the national church. This
church is known as the Igreja Missionaria (The Missionary Church).
We concentrate on the growth and development of the national
church because when the goal of an agency is to produce a church,
then "The only adequate basis of evaluation of mission is the
church produced on the field" (Johnson 1968:82). When viewed
as to the field results (as seen in its national church) the
Brazil history of the IMS divides into two periods which will be
treated in two sections: "The Twelve Years of Non-growth (1950-
1962)" and "The Six Years of Accelerated Church Growth (1962-
1967)".

Section I: The Twelve Years of Non-Growth

(1950-1962)

THE HISTORICAL ROOTS OF THE IMS IN JAPAN

Hear a parable! A seed must fall into the ground and die;
but if it die, it will bring forth much fruit. The history of
modern evangelical missions demonstrates that the indigenous
church is not only a praiseworthy ideal but the principal means
of fulfilling the global task we share with Christ of discipling
and perfecting a people for Himself.

The seed of God's Word that took root in the hearts of
Charles Cowman, Juji Nakada and Ernest A. Kilbourne (and in many
others later added to them) brought forth a hundred fold on
Japanese soil. What a strange team, it seems to us, God had
prepared in His perfect providence--two Christian telegraphers
and a Japanese student at Moody Bible Institute in Chicago, Illinois. All had their hearts set aflame for the evangelization
of Japan by one and the same Spirit.

On February 1, 1901, Charles Cowman and his wife, Lettie,
sailed from San Francisco and on the twenty-first of the same
month arrived in the land of their calling. Nakada was already
there to meet them. Within forty days Cowman and Nakada had
found and rented their first mission property in Tokyo (Duewel
1966:17).

As always God's timing was exact. The Cowmans began their
work in Japan in the first year of the outpouring of the Holy

Spirit in Japan which was a part of the larger world-wide revival of the first decade of the twentieth century (Orr 1965:
250). With prepared and revived lives Cowman and Nakada commen-
ced their work at the outset of a glorious movement of God's
Spirit that added 25,000 in twelve months to the Protestant forces in Japan (Orr 1965:250). In 1922, twenty one years later,
the Japan Holiness Church, the fruit of their labors, became
entirely indigenous (Duewel 1966:17).

Even in distant Brazil there were reverberations. The
early decades of the 1900's in Brazil saw an influx of Japanese
immigrants. By 1925 no less than 40,000 Japanese had settled
in Brazil by direct invitation of the government. The greater
part of these located in the state of Sao Paulo (Pierson 1925:
760).

Among these immigrants from Japan were some Christians, and
among these Christians was the Tanaami family, the first family
of the Japan Holiness Church to migrate to Brazil. In the month
of February, 1925 Hikozo, Takeuiro, and Shimekiti, three of
Haruzo Tanaami's four sons arrived in Sao Paulo (Interview,
Tanaami 1967). Haruzo had been converted to Christ in 1912
through the efforts of Juji Nakada (Elkjer 1967: Vol. LXVI, No.
4, 4), one of the co-founders of The Oriental Missionary Society
in Japan. Nakada himself later made a visit to Brazil where he
did evangelistic work (Interview, Pearson 1967). Haruzo had
participated in the Japan Every Creature Crusade , a systematic
home by home evangelism program, which was the burden and vision
of Charles Cowman (Elkjer 1967: Vol. LXVI, No. 4, 4). In five
years ten American Crusaders and ninety Japanese Christian workers blanketed systematically the whole nation of Japan with the
Gospel (Duewel 1966:10-11). This was a feat without precedent
and is perhaps without duplication in the annals of any other
nation of the world to date in such a thorough and comprehensive
manner.

The Tanaami brothers settled in Sao Paulo. Today, Tikara
Tanaami, the son of Hikozo, has a business office in the heart
of the city of Sao Paulo. Four blocks from this office is a
building with the placard, "Holiness Church," marking the place
of its beginnings in their adopted land (Interview, Pearson
1967). The Japanese Holiness Church in Brazil was formed in
1925 (Erny, Gillam, Elkjer 1957:8).

Takeo Monobe is the hero of the Japanese Holiness Church in
Brazil. In July, 1925 he came from Japan with that drive and
urgency that characterized Nakada, Cowman and Kilbourne and
others of the beginning days of the OMS. Many of the churches
and centers of the Brazil Japanese Holiness Church today were
established by the evangelistic work of Monobe. After some
brief time of passionate ministry he took ill and experienced
great pain and suffering. This illness began to interfere with
his evangelistic services; but he kept going. Wherever he went,
there was blessing and souls were saved. The infirmity finally

developed to the stage where he could no longer move, but never
did the passion to preach leave him. The Japanese would come
and crowd his room. There, in the midst of his agonies, close
to death, he was still preaching the unsearchable riches of
Christ (Interview, Pearson 1967). Monobe was trained in the OMS
Seminary in Tokyo and burned his life out in five years of service in Brazil. The Brazil Japanese Holiness Church was built
out of such heroic sacrifice (Pearson 1955: Vol. LIV, No. 7,4).
The churches founded by Takeo Monobe and others among the Japanese colonists of Brazil became autonomous in the year 1934 and
were renamed Igreja Holiness do Brasil (Holiness Church of Brazil) (Erny, Gillam, Elkjer 1957:8).

The Holiness Church of Brazil remained strictly a Japanese-
speaking church until World War II. "For awhile the Japanese
were not so popular in Brazil and could not continue their services in the Japanese language" (Pearson 1955: Vol. LIV, No. 7,
4). In 1943 the church in Presidente Prudente, Sao Paulo, engaged a Baptist layman, by the name of Joao Cantarin, to conduct
services in Portuguese. Thus was formed the first bi-cultural
IHB congregation later to be taken over by the Inter-American
Missionary Society (Correspondence, Elkjer 1967).

The story of the Brazil Japanese Holiness Church is a
thrilling but largely unknown chapter in the history of modern
evangelical missions. It is the account of a mission-related
church that became truly indigenous. The Brazil Japanese Holiness Church is in turn the product of the missionary concern and
effort of the Japan Holiness Church. Dr. B. H. Pearson who was
the first field director of the Inter-American Missionary Society work in Brazil quotes the people of the IHB as saying, "We
are not your children, but we are your grandchildren" (1955:
Vol. LIV, No. 7,4). Graph 10 illustrates the development of the
relationship of the Holiness Church to the Inter-American Missionary Society.

THE MISSION'S BRAZILIAN BEGINNINGS

Nestled in the hills near the bustling metropolis of
Sao Paulo, Brazil stood a rambling old American-type
home. Shouts of laughter rang through the rooms and
many little feet pattered the stairway. It was the
happy, busy home of "Mother" and "Daddy" Cooper--
American missionaries. But the little feet belonged
to Brazilian children.

Faithfully the little flock or orphans was ga-
thered for prayer each day. For a long time Mother
Cooper had been inspired and blessed by reading of
the Oriental Missionary Society in Japan. "We must
pray for those folks over there in Japan," she told

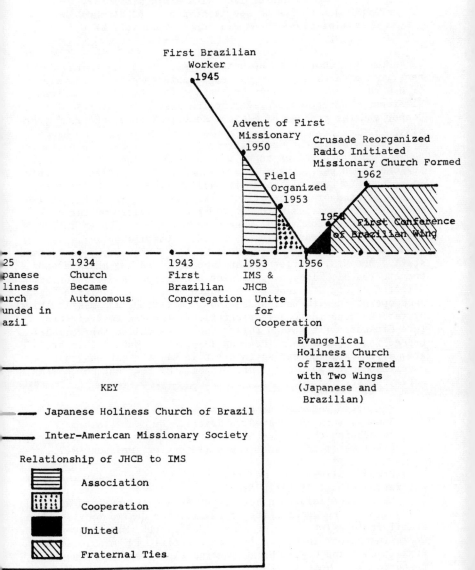

GRAPH 10

DIACHRONIC GRAPH OF SIGNIFICANT DATES

OF THE JAPANESE HOLINESS CHURCH

AND THE INTER-AMERICAN MISSIONARY SOCIETY WORKS

First Brazilian
Worker
1945

Advent of First
Missionary
1950

Crusade Reorganized
Radio Initiated
Missionary Church Formed
1962

Field
Organized
1953

1956

First Conference
of Brazilian Wing

25
panese
liness
urch
unded in
azil

1934
Church
Became
Autonomous

1943
First
Brazilian
Congregation

1953
IMS &
JHCB
Unite
for
Cooperation

1956

Evangelical
Holiness Church
of Brazil Formed
with Two Wings
(Japanese and
Brazilian)

KEY

Japanese Holiness Church of Brazil

Inter-American Missionary Society

Relationship of JHCB to IMS

Association

Cooperation

United

Fraternal Ties

the children. . . And pray they did!
    Then one day a new conviction was born in the
heart of Mother Cooper. "We need this kind of missionary work here in Brazil. We must pray for the
Oriental Missionary Society to come here." . . .
    Thirty years later those prayers were answered,
although the wonderful lady with a big missionary
heart did not live to see it happen. But her husband
and some of the orphans did (Erny 1965: Vol. LXIV,
No. 11,17).

How like God! When He determines to do a new thing, He often first creates a desire to see it come to pass in the hearts
of His children. Brazilian beginnings for the Inter-American
Missionary Society were prayer beginnings in the hearts of Mother
Cooper and the orphans of Blossom Home in Suzano, Sao Paulo, Brazil.
    The unfolding of God's answer to those orphans' prayers re-
veals a providential pattern, the whole of which was veiled to
any one human participant. Each knew his own part and a little
more, but God knew all, and His will was the unifying factor.
    A great door in the Orient snapped shut. In China, in 1941,
many OMS missionaries were put under house arrest by the Japanese who occupied China. They were transferred to an intern-
ment camp in the early months of 1942 (Duewel 1966:14). It
appeared that the work being done by the OMS had come to a stand-
still. But Mrs. Charles Cowman, who survived her husband and
perpetuated his missionary passion and vision, had already been
directed of God "to look to the south land." In 1941 she began,
in cooperation with Mexican national Christians and missionaries
of various denominational orientations, the Mexico Every Creature Crusade. (In Mexico this crusade was called the National
Evangelistic Campaign.) (Pearson 1961:160). Out of this crusade
grew a general, increasing interest in all the nations that lay
under the Southern Cross. Dr. Benjamin H. Pearson, her co-la-
borer, says:

    She often referred to the lands of the Southern Cross.
    She was much interested in Brazil. We often talked
    concerning the land and the early martyrs of the be-
    ginnings of the Gospel there (Interview, Pearson 1967).

Mrs. Cowman believed she had discovered God's plan for the evangelization of all of Latin America.
    "Since she laid down her armour at eighty years of age in
1949, she had no opportunity to fulfill her desire to visit the
Brazil field" (Interview, Pearson 1967). Yet, Mrs. Cowman was
God's instrument in the calling of the first IMS missionaries to
Brazil, Carl and Gracie Hahn. During the time that Hahn was
pastoring Rees Memorial Church in Pasadena, California, Mrs.

Hahn relates the following experience:

> We entertained in our church The Oriental Missionary
> Society for their Annual Convention, at which time we
> heard Mrs. Cowman tell again the thrilling story of
> the growth of the Society, and of its advance into
> South America. During her message she said, and never
> will I forget her words!--"We are now ready to open
> the work in Brazil, and are praying for a *God-called*
> and *prepared* man to supervise the work there." Some-
> thing like a dagger hit my heart, and I cried out,
> "Oh God, is this the secret why we have been hin-
> dered from entering any other open door to the mis-
> sionary field?" I knew it was. It was like a cur-
> tain pulled aside and there was a clear open road,
> leading right to Brazil (1950: Vol. XLIX, Vol. 9,
> 5 & 17).

Though the Hahns were the first IMS missionaries to work in
Brazil, they did not make the first contact for the society.
During the war in the spring of 1942, Dr. Roy Adams and Rev. C.
P. Culver made a survey trip through South America. They visited Brazil and recommended it as a second field of missionary
occupation by the society (Interview, Adams 1968). Even before
this survey trip, Dr. George Ridout, an evangelist and professor
from Asbury College, held meetings in Brazil (Erny 1965: Vol.
LXIV, No. 11,17). One of his contacts was Rev. Jonathas Thomas
de Aquino, a national pastor and seminary professor of the Congregational Church, who experienced what he felt was a holiness
experience and wanted to be associated with the OMS (Interview,
Pearson 1967). After a visit from the OMS representative,
Charles P. Culver (Erny 1965: Vol. LXIV, No. 11,17), Rev. Jonathas Thomas de Aquino became a national co-worker in Brazil,
supported by the society. He worked in this capacity for five
years before the arrival of the Hahns in 1950 (Editor's note,
Aquino 1950: Vol. XLIX, No. 11,5). During these years, Rev.
Jonathas had a successful evangelistic ministry characterized
by the calling of young people into Christian service and prepared the way for the IMS missionaries. In later years he was
a professor in the IMS Bible Institute and Seminary in Londrina,
Parana. "Dadinho," as he is affectionately called, was also for
some years Superintendent of the national church (Interview,
Pearson 1967) and editor of the Brazil edition of the IMS revival magazine, *Reavivamento*. "Dadinho" is one of Brazil's living,
spiritual giants. Dr. B. H. Pearson says of his fatherly preaching which he witnessed in Londrina, Parana,

> He would ask people to come forward to be prayed with.
> A large portion of the audience would come up. He
> would place his hands on their shoulders and look up

to heaven and pray for God's blessing to fall on them
and His Spirit to fill them. It was very moving and
beautiful, indeed (1967).

THE ARRIVAL OF THE FIRST IMS MISSIONARIES (1950)

Carl Hahn, preceding his family, left New York by ship June
7, 1950 (The Oriental Missionary Society 1950: Vol. XLIX, No. 7,
12) and on Sunday evening, the twenty-fifth of the same month,
was anchored in the harbor of Rio de Janeiro (Hahn 1950a: Vol.
XLIX, No. 8,9). It was too late to clear customs. On the docks
waited Rev. Jonathas Thomas de Aquino and his Brazilian friends
to welcome the first IMS missionary to Brazil (Hahn 1950a: Vol.
XLIX, No. 8,9).

Who was this new missionary? What group did he represent?
What was his purpose in Brazil? Such were surely some of the
questions that would soon arise in the minds of many in the Evangelical community of Brazil.

In 1957 the IMS published formally in Portuguese a statement of its doctrinal position which had previously been commun-
icated by witness and proclamation: the plenary inspiration of
the whole Bible, the Trinity, the fall of man and his resultant
moral depravity, the necessity of the new birth; the expiation
of sin by the blood of Christ, justification by faith; sanctifi-
cation by faith subsequent to the new birth, wrought by the infilling of the Holy Spirit, resulting in heart purity and power
for life and service; divine healing as a Christian's privilege;
the resurrection of the body; the second premillenial coming of
Christ; eternal life of the saved and eternal punishment of the
lost (Erny, Gillam, Elkjer 1957:10). A fuller statement of the
doctrinal position can be found in *The Missionary Standard,* the
official publication of the Oriental Missionary Society. The
Society's doctrinal uniqueness lies in the emphasis upon santi-
fication as an experience of the infilling of the Holy Spirit
subsequent to the new birth which purifies the heart of the be-
liever and empowers him to live a holy life and fulfill his
Christian service. It was this emphasis upon the second defi-
nite work of grace that distinguished the mission from most but
not all other Evangelical agencies in Brazil.

What was the purpose of this missionary and the mission he
represented? Rev. Carl Hahn writing shortly after his arrival
in Brazil said,

> Our program will be the same as that followed in other
> [OMS] fields--direct evangelism with a three-fold em-
> phasis:
>
> 1. The training of the nationals . . . . This
>   calls for strategically-located . . . Bible
>   Seminaries.

      2. The establishment of a truly indigenous
         church . . .
      3. Organizing Every Creature Crusades (1950:
    Vol. XLIX, No. 7,12 & 19).

Carl Hahn, IMS Superintendent for Brazil (Editor's note, Hahn 1950: Vol. XLIX, No. 7,12), found a warm Brazilian welcome waiting as he disembarked and set foot for the first time on Brazilian soil. This first meeting now seems prophetic of the many friends God gave the society in its new field in answer to the orphans' prayers.

Hahn reports only one year after his arrival in Brazil:

> The work of the Inter-American Missionary Society now
> includes a Bible House . . ., a full time colporteur,
> three organized churches, several additional preaching
> points, a radio program, Spiritual Life Conventions
> and evangelistic meetings, in addition to the Every
> Creature Crusade (Hahn 1951: Vol. L, No. 10,5).

Although there was some distribution of the Scriptures mostly among the Japanese immigrants, this report of Crusade should not be confused with the Japan or Mexico or other national Crusades. In fact, this regional effort never really got off the ground.

Dr. B. H. Pearson reports on the work after visiting Brazil in 1951 and helps explain the apparently phenomenal growth and development,

We become heirs of
    1. A ready-made Japanese Conference of Holiness
       Churches of Brazil. [This church had been
       autonomous since 1934.]
    2. Three good church buildings and congregations
       of Brazilian people.
    3. The Bible House in Londrina.
    4. More preaching points and possible centers
       than we can possibly man at present, radi-
       ating out from the above centers.
    5. A Brazil which welcomes the Protestant
       preacher and missionary.
    6. A splendid group of Christian youth who with
       Bible training will become sturdy leaders of
       our church tomorrow (Pearson 1951: Vol. L,
    No. 11, 5 & 16).

Heirs. Yes, God had opened the hearts of many and had given them as friends to the IMS. During that visit, Dr. B. H. Pearson attended the Spiritual Life Conference in Suzano, Sao Paulo, whose president was the same Carl ("Daddy") Cooper of the Blossom Home orphanage, and reported,

It [the conference] was held in the Suzano Church, a
beautiful building, with seating capacity for some two
hundred or more people. This property is owned by the
congregation, but the congregation has accepted our
doctrinal statement. We are giving some slight assistance to the pastor, and the congregation is ours as
we form a Brazilian Church (Pearson 1951: Vol. L, No.
11,5).

The IMS became heirs also of the Spiritual Life Conference.
Gracie Hahn writes in late 1952,

The communion service on Sunday morning was conducted
by "Daddy" Cooper, now eighty-three years of age. It
was a touching and blessed time, especially when he
stood with his arms around Mr. Hahn giving him his
blessing and praying for our work in Brazil, then
announcing that he was turning the responsibility of
his churches and the Spiritual Life Convention to
Mr. Hahn and the Inter-American Missionary Society
(1952a: Vol. LI, No. 12, 8 & 15).

Rev. Roderick Davies was another such benefactor of the IMS.
Rev. Davies, a Plymouth Brethren missionary in Londrina, Parana,
had been for years a friend of the society and had patterned his
work after the OMS. Dr. B. H. Pearson reports concerning the
large role Rev. Davies played in the beginnings of the society's
work in Brazil,

It could not have been possible for the OMS to place
missionaries in Brazil except through and as a part
of some existing organization. . . . He [Rev. Davies]
opened the doors to Brazil for us, invited us in, and
turned over to us his work (1951: Vol. L, No. 11, 5 &
16).

This work included a Bible House and two churches, the Avenida
Parana Church in Londrina and a church in Iguaracu, all in the
north of the state of Parana. There was yet another notable
contribution made by Rev. Davies to the IMS a few years later.
One of his converts was Ayrton Justus who is now General Superintendent of the Inter-American Missionary Society's national
church (Interview, Pearson 1967).

Perhaps it was the "grandchildren" that helped the society
the most in the early days in the new field. There was from the
outset of Hahn's work the closest co-operation on the part of
the Japanese Holiness Church of Brazil. Gracie Hahn tells of
ministering to the children in the Japanese Sunday School where
fifty of the one hundred children responded to an invitation to
confess their sins and to accept Christ as personal Savior (Hahn
1952: Vol. LI, No. 1, 5 & 16).

The dates, January 4 through 19, 1953, mark an historic
conference which was held in the city of Presidente Prudente,
Sao Paulo, where pastors and representatives of fifteen of the
Holiness Churches of Brazil under the leadership of Bishop
Shimekiti Tanaami, met with Rev. Carl Hahn, for the purpose of
uniting their work with the work of the Inter-American Missionary Society. Bishop Shimekiti Tanaami wrote Dr. B. H. Pearson:

> The two great purposes of the work of our church at the
> present moment have been and are the evangelization of
> the people of this nation and also the evangelization
> of the entire South American Continent . . . I am es-
> pecially pleased with the decision made in our recent
> assembly . . . . At that time our church united with
> The Oriental Missionary Society of the Inter-American
> Missionary Society with the fundamental objective of
> evangelizing Brazil (Pearson 1953: Vol. LII, No. 4,7).

Carl Hahn had an effective evangelistic ministry during
those years. Dr. B. H. Pearson related that he preached with
"much unction"--that is, with a great sense of the presence of
God and a deep interest in people (Interview, Pearson 1967). He
had in the first year on the field acquired a facility with the
Portuguese language though over forty years old (Pearson 1951:
Vol. L, No. 11, 5). Mrs. Hahn reports that on a 1951 trip to
the interior, Carl preached seventeen times in ten days with
over 100 persons being saved (1951a: Vol. LII, No. 10,5). In
1952 Carl Hahn worked with Dr. J. Edwin Orr in his outstanding
revival ministry. Carl would go into a city and invite all the
pastors to a dinner or luncheon, present them the pattern and
program, get interest started and prayer going, and get the pastors to set up the meetings (Interview, Pearson 1967).

To present a complete picture of the reception the IMS received in Brazil we need to fill in between the bright shades of
friendship, help and co-operation, the darker shade--the opposi-
tion of most Evangelicals at that time to the formation of any
new denomination in Brazil. Dr. Pearson, who was the founding
director of the IMS in Brazil, was advised by the Executive Secretary of the Evangelical Confederation of Brazil not to found
a new denomination inasmuch as there were too many denominations
already. Dr. Pearson took this suggestion seriously and began
to investigate the possibility of developing a Brazilian wing of
the Holiness Church (Correspondence, Elkjer 1967). In reflec-
tion, Dr. Pearson says,

> New groups [denominations] have come in and continue to
> come in. . . The population continue to grow by mil-
> lions every year, so any new mission has a few extra
> million to work on in addition to her tens of millions
> that no other church has yet evangelized (Interview,
> Pearson 1967).

REORGANIZING TO BUILD (1953-1961)

Though at the very first the Hahns were the only IMS missionaries in the country, reinforcements arrived in 1951, 1952 and a larger contingent in 1953 (Duewel 1966:24). In 1953 prior to the Hahn's transfer to another mission, there were five missionary families on the field. It was the year of reorganization.

A new constitution has been adopted by the Oriental Missionary Society in 1949 providing for the establishment of a field executive committee. The field executive committee was designed to give younger missionaries a share in decision-making on the field.

> This constitution did not please every one of the OMS field directors. It meant for some that their authority was being limited but not necessarily the responsibility which the director had to carry before the board. This was something some directors found difficult to fit into while others found joy in this sharing. It did mean, however, that where the OMS had been losing its younger leadership previously and in some places was in dire straights. . ., that there began an increase in younger leadership that has produced the OMS of our day (Interview, Pearson 1967).

Dr. Eugene Erny, President of the OMS, and William Gillam visited the Brazil field at this time, and Dr. Erny presided over the meeting in which the Brazil IMS missionaries elected their first field executive committee. Dr. Pearson, now in residence in Brazil at this time, was therefore able to take up the direction of the field in association with this new committee.

In the fall of 1953 the property for the Bible Institute was purchased. This is a thrilling story in its own right of God's guidance and provision. There was a need for a school to train Brazilian Christian workers; but beyond that, the missionaries needed such an effort around which to rally. Dr. B. H. Pearson reflects,

> We had at that time a group of missionaries who felt that their efforts had been dissipated--that they were scattered in rather meaningless positions without relationship to raising up a field. That was one of the great needs. . . to have some goal and some task that they could take hold of and feel they were going somewhere (Interview 1967).

To meet these needs, the search for God's location began. "Maringa was the place that our brother, Carl Hahn, had urgently advocated as the center for the Bible School" (Interview, Pearson 1967). Maringa was the city that was viewed as the coming center of the new Brazilian frontier and of the great coffee empire that seemed inevitable for the area. The IMS owned a piece of property, but it was covered with jungle and at least a mile from any street with the semblance of rock in it. It was totally inaccessible in the rainy season. There was another problem. The society had $12,000 with which to begin the operation of the Bible School. Dr. B. H. Pearson observes, "Twelve thousand dollars could not have put us into operation, even in thatched huts, in Maringa" (Interview 1967).

Missionary Rev. Robert Millan was at that time living in the Bible House in Londrina. He had made contact with the Evangelical pastors and leaders of Londrina. He also knew Dr. Zaqueu de Mello of the Filadelfia School and the Londrinense College. Out of these contacts and the confidence of these men in Robert Millan came the willingness of Dr. Zaqueu de Mello to sell the property of the Filadelfia School to the IMS.

In the missionary meetings held at this time it was taken for granted that the city of Sao Paulo should be the location of the Bible School. A church was offered as a place where classes could be held to get started. Then, on the last afternoon of these meetings, Robert Millan presented the possibilities of Londrina and Dr. Zaqueu's offer to sell the property. It had only one drawback. Only $12,000 were available and the price was $22,000! A few days later the Treasurer at the mission headquarters sent a balance sheet showing that the Brazil Building Fund now had $18,500. Dr. Pearson gives this thrilling account of his dealings with Dr. Zaqueu:

> I told him our dilemma as the OMS at that time did not
> enter into indebtedness, did not give mortgage or a
> trust deed on a property. He said to me, "That's
> alright, Dr. Pearson. Give me the $18,500 and I will
> give you a clear and unencumbered title to the prop-
> erty. You can pay me the rest of it when and as you
> get it." I have never been trusted by anyone in any
> country such as that (Interview 1967).

There was more building to be done on the property and Rev. Howard Hill who had previous experience in missionary building projects in China and Japan was appointed to Brazil to supervise the construction.

When the Bible Institute and Seminary of Londrina opened in March, 1954 (Duewel 1966:24), it was on an inter-denominational basis (Correspondence, Elkjer 1967).

> The Independent Presbyterian pastor came in to the
> school as a regular teacher as did the Methodist
> pastor. Senhor Francisco Vieira, a Presbyterian

> layman, came in to act as builder and counselor. He
> and his wife served as dean of men and dean of women.
> So then with those who came in from other churches,
> faith was kept; and no attempt was ever made to sway
> them [the students] into the orbit of the OMS (Inter-
> view, Pearson 1967).

The Bible Institute and Seminary of Londrina had a part in the
training of some outstanding Brazilian pastors of the Independent Presbyterian and Baptist churches. And the Holiness Church
of Brazil adopted it as its official training school (Erny, Gillam, Elkjer 1957:8).

It was in 1956 that the Holiness Church was reorganized as
two wings, Japanese and Brazilian, under one general denomination. "The Brazilian wing held its first annual conference and
organized itself in January, 1958 with the participation of
churches in Maringa, Iguaracu, Presidente Prudente and Suzano"
(Correspondence, Elkjer 1967). In the year 1959 the Brazilian
wing of the Holiness Church had 310 communicant members; next
year it fell to 273 members but again by 1962 it had grown to
349 members. Thus, the net gain in three years, as can be seen
in Graph 11, was only thirty-nine members.

FACTORS INHIBITING GROWTH

What were the major factors that served to inhibit the
growth of the church related to the IMS during the first twelve
years of its missionary effort in south Brazil?

1. The Absence of Clear-cut Church-Planting Goals. Rev.
Carl Hahn was obviously a gifted evangelist. For example, there
were the one hundred persons brought to saving faith in Jesus
Christ on the ten-day preaching itinerary. Nevertheless no new
churches were begun in the interior by the IMS during that time
which survive to the present. Furthermore, much of the work of
the early missionaries was of an interdenominational nature.
Carl Hahn, for example, was extensively involved in 1952 in the
revival ministry of J. Edwin Orr.

Certainly there were results through the gifted and conse-
crated lives of these early IMS missionaries that eternity alone
will tell. But in terms of congregations founded, local churches
organized and communicant members added in IMS related churches,
little tangible results remain. Apparently this was not a
clear-cut goal. By 1953 there were five IMS families in Brazil.
Some were sent into the interior with little or no language
training (Interview, Pearson 1967). These new missionaries were
for the most part in confusion and "felt that their efforts were
dissipated--that they were scattered in rather meaningless po-
sitions. . ." (Interview, Pearson 1967).

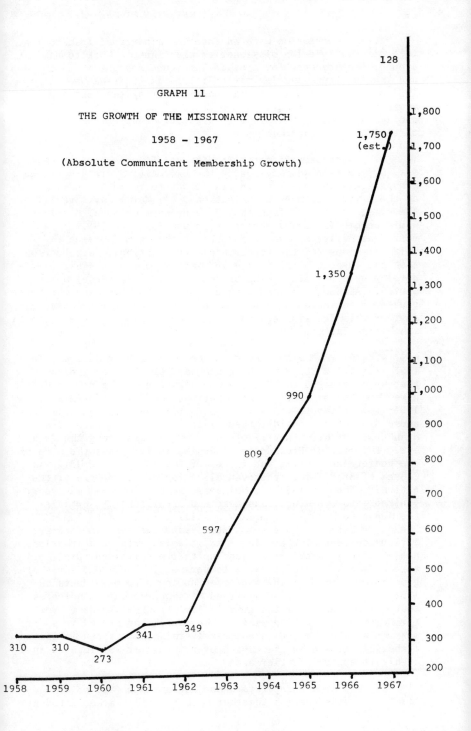

GRAPH 11

THE GROWTH OF THE MISSIONARY CHURCH

1958 - 1967

(Absolute Communicant Membership Growth)

2. *Preoccupation with an Interdenominational Institution.*
In order that the IMS missionaries might have a work to rally
around, the property for a Bible Institute was purchased in 1953
and the Instituto and Seminario Biblico de Londrina opened in
1954 on an interdenominational basis. During the next eight
years the IMS missionaries were largely committed to staffing
and administrating the mission institution and caring for the
three inherited churches.

3. *Resistance from the Traditional Denominations.* As we
saw, Dr. Pearson was advised by the Executive Secretary of the
Evangelical Confederation in Brazil not to found a denomination
as there were too many denominations. J. Merle Davis verifies
the existence of the fear that "the undenominational missions"
would become or create sectarian groups (1943:84,85). It appears that distrust was reciprocal at that time between the
faith missions and the traditional denominations. Dr. Pearson
took the suggestion seriously and turned to the possibility of
developing a Brazilian wing of the existing (Japanese) Holiness
Church. Although this must have appeared to have been the best
course of action open to the IMS at that time, the negative result of this decision can be seen as we consider the next growth
inhibiting factor.

4. *The Yoke with a Foreign Homogeneous Unit Church.* In a
1951 article in *The Missionary Standard* Dr. Pearson indicates
that he considered the "ready-made Japanese Conference of Holiness Churches of Brazil" the inheritance of the IMS (Pearson
1951: Vol. L, No. 11, 5 & 16). But it is certain that the Japanese did not so consider themselves. As early as 1952 Gracie
Hahn tells of her ministry of child evangelism among the Japanese. The city of Presidente Prudente, in 1953, was the site of
the conference uniting the forces of the IMS and the Holiness
Church of Brazil for "the evangelization of the people of the
nation." Then in 1956 the Holiness Church of Brazil was reorganized into two wings, Japanese and Brazilian. Nevertheless
the Japanese Holiness Church was still largely that--Japanese.
Preaching services have sometimes passed through two interpre-
tations to reach the people. And it is apparent that the Japanese share with the Brazilians neither a common cultural heritage nor their characteristic temperament. The great surge of
growth registered by the increased number of communicants in
1963 over 1962 in the newly-freed Missionary Church indicates
that the dominance of the numerically stronger Japanese over
the Portuguese-speaking wing of the church had served in some
measure as a brake. Unintentionally this association inhibited
membership growth in the church even though it was located in a
highly receptive frontier area.

5. *The Continuing Interdenominational Concept of Evangelism.* The missionaries together with the Bible School students

carried out various efforts of evangelism--all of which were interdenominational in nature. Most popular of these efforts were the "caravans" held at the completion of a six-week unit of study. Students under missionary direction would visit a town and conduct a three-day campaign during which the students would put into practice the methods and ideas learned in their study period. The potential contribution of this effort to church growth was totally dependent upon follow-up by local churches of various denominations.

A further example of this type of interdenominatiônal evangelism was the missionary-directed evangelistic Crusade conducted in 1956 in the city of Maringa. This extended campaign used a team of Bible school students called "Crusaders." The Crusaders sought to channel the new converts into local churches but they often found that the pastors were too busy with their own congregations. One team member, Ayrton Justus, went back the following year in an effort to conserve the fruits of evangelism and establish a church but could only locate two individuals that were won to faith in Christ through the Crusade effort. Rev. Justus tells of preaching many a Sunday with only his wife as a congregation in an attempt to get a church started at the former Crusade location. Through the persistent faithfulness of Rev. Justus in a receptive frontier city this Maringa church which had such a poor beginning has now become the strongest local congregation in the denomination.

Some of the fruit from these interdenominational evangelistic efforts became local churches of other denominations. One example is the second largest Baptist congregation in the city of Londrina that resulted from a ministry carried on by the Bible Institute students under missionary direction. While this congregation did not help to build up the national church related to the IMS, its existence is proof of the great value, potentially, of the type of evangelization carried out by the students in their practical work.

6. *Church Planting Dependent on Nationals.* Because the IMS missionaries were involved in administrating the Bible Institute, maintaining the inherited churches and carrying out programs of interdenominational evangelism, the opportunity to plant churches of their own denomination passed them by. It was not until nationals (some of whom were being trained in the Londrina Bible Institute and others who would join them later) could take the lead in establishing and developing churches, that the denomination related to the IMS would begin its more recent pattern of good church growth.

Section II: The Six Years of Accelerated
Church Growth (1962-1967)

The Missionary Church since 1962 has been experiencing an
accelerated average annual growth rate of 38 per cent. It is
growing at 345 per cent of the national annual average for Evangelical communicants in Brazil. What are the circumstances sur-
rounding and the factors effecting the shift from a static
church to one of growth? There has of course been some build up
of the missionary staff--twenty-five missionaries in 1969 over
against ten in 1953--but as has been noted in the previous chapter, only two of the twenty-five in 1969 were deployed church
planters. To this small number of designated church planters
must be linked the interdenominational and institutional preoccupation of IMS missionaries described in the previous section.
Thus the build up of missionary personnel is not in itself adequate to explain such a drastic change in the growth pattern of
this mission-related church.

THE NEW BEGINNING

The most colorful and perhaps the most important year in
the history of the Inter-American Missionary Society in Brazil
was 1962. Charles Elkjer writes of the conditions that surround-
ed a gracious revival visitation of God which has largely shaped
the subsequent work and organizational relationships of the IMS
in Brazil:

> At this time, [August, 1961] with the resignation from
> the presidency of Janio Quadros, the nation was plunged
> into a military crisis which threatened a civil war to
> prevent Communist-inclined Joao Goulart's succession to
> the presidency. A peaceful solution was found through
> a parlimentary form of government which gave Goulart
> the office with reduced power [a tactical move which
> postponed the violent military-Goulart confrontation
> until 1964]. During this crisis when it appeared that
> our door of ministry in Brazil might close, God began
> to speak to us of this vast nation, still largely un-
> reached with its many facets of need. When anguished
> hours of tension gave way to joyful peace, an over-
> whelming sense of gratitude filled our hearts to find
> ourselves still in Brazil, as it were, "alive from
> the dead," and facing a wide, wide open door with a
> sense of urgency. . . . This led to a week of spe-
> cial thanksgiving and prayer on the part of our
> missionaries in which . . . we were led to place our

entire mission operation on the altar with the
prayer that if God saw fit He might revolutionize
our work in order to use us in some way toward
reaching all of Brazil quickly while there was
time (1965).

That it was indeed God's revival is seen by the fact that missionaries, national workers and Bible School students were melt-
ed together in a new love-unity in Christ.

It was soon realized that if the Brazilian wing of the Holiness Church was to take advantage of its opportunity and see
rapid church growth, it would be necessary to separate from the
Japanese wing of the Holiness Church (Duewel 1966:25). This
realization resulted in an amicable separation effected in 1962
after which both groups continued to maintain fraternal ties.
The Brazilian wing was renamed Igreja Missionaria (The Missionary Church) (Elkjer 1965). The new denomination was organized
along autonomous lines similar to its mother church and formed
a new constitution patterned after that of the IMS national
church in Colombia, South America (see Plate 7, Organizational
Structure of National Church).

In the first year of its new denominational life the Missionary Church experienced a 41.8 per cent increase in membership (see Graph 11). Every area of the church's life was pro-
foundly affected. It was a great leap forward in which two
churches were organized, fourteen congregations founded, thirty-
six preaching points opened, 146 believers baptized, 248 members
added to the denomination, thirteen Sunday Schools opened and
362 Sunday School students enrolled (The Oriental Missionary
Society 1964:5).

THE TWO MAJOR FACTORS INVOLVED IN THE
ACCELERATED GROWTH OF THE MISSIONARY CHURCH

The first factor was the new spiritual dynamic that entered
the lives of national and missionary alike because of the revival visitation of God. Not only was a new unity experienced,
but a new passion for evangelism was born which was shared by
national and missionary alike.

A second factor, however, was purely mechanical: the separation of the Portuguese-speaking, or shall we say European
wing from the older, Japanese Holiness Church. It produced a
young church that was free to answer the challenge and opportunity afforded it in the massive Portuguese population of Brazil.
This new-found independence was consistently carried over into
the new denomination. The new church, which is characterized
by strong national leadership, is autonomous. The decision-
making power was placed almost wholly in the control of national
leaders, and the mission continues to provide financial support

PLATE 7

ORGANIZATIONAL STRUCTURE OF NATIONAL CHURCH

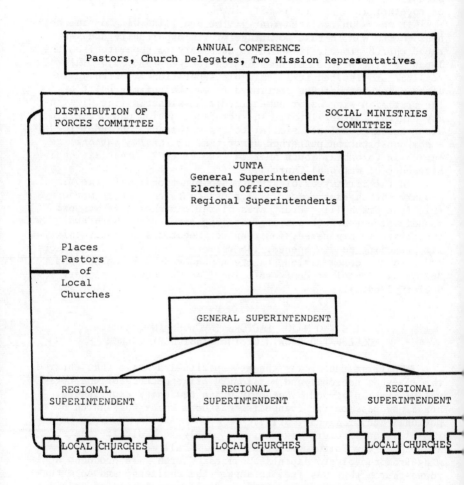

to subsidize national workers with an aim to eventual self-support. This was a crucial decision, correctly made. For had a new mission domination been substituted for the previous complete independence of the Brazil Holiness Church, there would likely be no accelerated church growth to report.

IMS missionaries, in recognizing that "among the many aspects of human society none is more important than these homogeneous units of mankind" (McGavran 1965:69), operated according to established church growth principles in the separation of the Brazilian and Japanese wings of the Holiness Church. McGavran gives three principles concerning the homogeneous unit church all of which were involved in the creation of the parallel churches:

1) Each homogeneous unit church has its own measure of responsiveness to the Christian message.
2) Each homogeneous unit church flourishes best under its own leaders.
3) Each denomination in each homogeneous unit of the general population needs its own church organization (1969:77,79).

In the final analysis not one but two churches were freed to experience their own greatest growth potential. This is not to say that some day a bi-cultural denomination will not be desirable but that day will not come until Brazil enjoys a larger degree of homogeneity in its own general population. Until that time we dare not fail to recognize the homogeneous units within the general population and claim them for Christ.

TWO MISSION INNOVATIONS EMERGING FROM THE REVIVAL

The revival time was also a time of innovation of new specialized ministries by the mission. Crusade evangelism was launched and the use of radio as a possible means of spreading the Gospel throughout Brazil impressed itself on the minds of the missionaries. Today *"Ondas de Paz"* ("Waves of Peace"), a seven-day-a-week radio program reaches a major portion of Brazil's population on fifteen radio stations (Correspondence, Wolff 1967). Thus, plans born of God-given urgency in the midst of the revival became a reality.

The Crusade. The Crusade was a program of direct evangelism which entailed the distribution of Scripture portions house by house, personal witnessing and nightly evangelistic meetings.

As Dr. B. H. Pearson left the work of the OMS [IMS] in Londrina in 1955, his last two messages to the students were on the Every Creature Crusades in Japan and Mexico, which planted seeds that germinated in burning hearts that gave birth to the first Crusade effort on

the Brazil field. Under the direction of Clarence
Owsley, a campaign (1956) was launched that covered
the city of Maringa in six months. Other campaigns
were held in Cambe and Londrina in Vila Nova [all
in the north of the Brazilian state of Parana].
Although there was not sufficient personnel to continue the Crusade at that time, the Crusade vision
was permanently planted in hearts of both national
workers and students and missionaries (Elkjer 1965).

The Japan Every Creature Crusade covered the nation in
house to house Scripture distribution by using teams of nationals led by a missionary Crusader. In Japan the OMS was so bent
on the coverage of the nation and at the same time so unprepared
for the conversion of great numbers of people, that wherever
possible the converts were channeled into existing churches and
some young congregations were turned over to other evangelical
groups which could supply pastors. We are not here trying to
devaluate this early Every Creature Crusade but merely to show
the concept of Crusade that existed in the minds of IMS missionaries. Crusade then was to the IMS missionary a thrilling program of Scripture distribution and direct evangelism of national
proportions which did not necessarily include the establishment
of local churches or a denomination.

In 1959 the missionaries prayed about the future of some
capable students and graduates who were not committed to any
mission or denomination. "God's answer came in one word--'Crusade'" (Elkjer 1965). It was announced by faith that Crusade
would be resumed in 1960. This announcement was made without
promise of personnel or finances. Unknown to the missionaries,
this group of nationals, together with some others, had banded
together to pray for the evangelization of northern Parana and
had resolved to undertake some type of direct evangelism. There
was sufficient nationalism at that time to prevent some of the
students from working in a mission-directed Crusade program.
Then came the revival visitation in which workers and missionaries were given a new oneness of spirit and purpose. Thereupon
workers of the Brazilian wing of the Holiness Church launched a
new crusade-type ministry called "Operation Evangelism." This
new effort under national leadership was without a missionary
Crusader. Rudolf Friesen and Geraldo Klassen labored heroically
for two years without a means of transportation and with very
little financial help (Elkjer 1965).

Then in 1962 at a special General Conference, convened for
the purpose of forming a constitution for the new church body,
Missionary Austin Boggan was invited by national leaders to take
over the direction of the Crusade. The Crusade was renamed *A
Cruzada das Boas Novas* (The Good News Crusade). This Good News
Crusade was mission-financed and under the direction of a *junta*
with national and missionary representation.

But it remained for nationals to envision the Crusade as a church-planting arm of the Missionary Church. In 1966, when the writer was director of the Crusade, there existed a partial conflict between the understanding of the leaders of the national church and the understanding of some missionaries as to what the principal purpose of Crusade was to be. IMS missionaries emerged from the 1961 national emergency feeling that perhaps their days of opportunity for reaching the multitudes in Brazil were numbered. Their response to the crisis was to begin the radio broadcasts with a goal of total national coverage and to perpetuate a concept of the Crusade based largely on the Japan Every Creature Crusade. The director, at that time, Austin Boggan, had first served as a missionary Crusader in the Orient. In the early 1960's the purpose was to spread the Gospel as fast as possible. If churches were raised up in the wake of the Crusade, so much the better. But to most missionaries the Crusade was not readily seen as the church-planting arm of the national church. In 1968 the Missionary Church founded (in a vacuum left by the "temporary disbanding and reforming" of the Good News Crusade) its own Crusade which is currently working in the state of Mato Grosso. The new national Crusade, although financed directly from the United States, is independent of missionary direction. The fully developed form that the national Crusade will take remains to be seen, but we can be sure that its goal is to plant Missionary Churches.

The missionary-directed Crusade (*Cruzada das Boas Novas*) is currently concentrating on Brazil's great industrial complex, Sao Paulo. Two missionaries were deployed there in 1969 to plant churches in the *bairros* (outlying districts) that circle the city and constitute its growing edge due to the influx of migrants from the North.

Radio. The daily IMS radio broadcast, even more than the Crusade, has become an outlet for the missionary's concept of interdenominational mission. The missionaries' conception of the radio broadcast as an interdenominational evangelistic ministry of nation-wide proportions has served to obscure its potential in aiding the national church to grow.

The effective use of radio by Pentecostal pastors for church extension and development clearly points out the possibility for pastors and workers of the Missionary Church. In Brazil radio is used by churches not only as a preaching medium but live broadcasts are used to tie remote congregations to mother churches and often serve as a one-way telephone to tell of special events, communicate personal greetings and messages and to advise of pastoral and evangelistic visits. There is much that Brazilians can teach us concerning the use of radio as an effective tool of local churches. IMS missionaries involved in radio ministry need to study how others are using radio to help local churches grow. They should explore new avenues

KEY

Churches Planted by:

● Missionaries
+ Crusade workers
x National Churchmen
* Churches Inherited

MATO GROSSO

Source: Deggau 1967

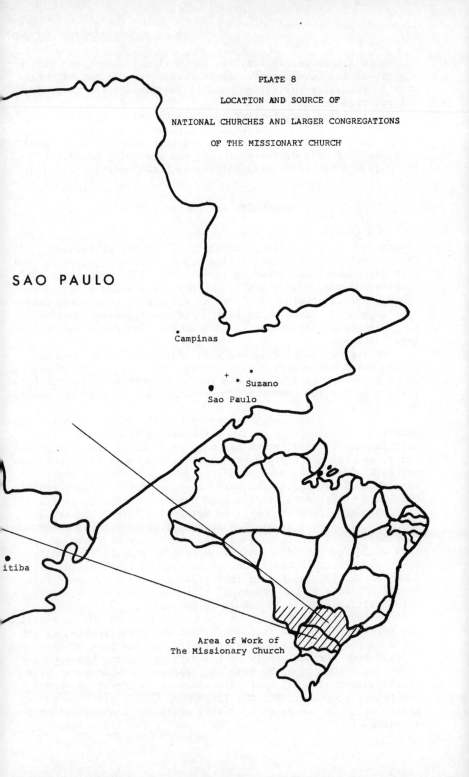

PLATE 8

LOCATION AND SOURCE OF

NATIONAL CHURCHES AND LARGER CONGREGATIONS

OF THE MISSIONARY CHURCH

SAO PAULO

Campinas

Suzano
Sao Paulo

itiba

Area of Work of
The Missionary Church

through which to relate radio to the national church and aid in
its growth and development. To do this, it would not be necessary to sacrifice the vision born in the revival for total Brazil coverage.

A Brazilian scriptwriter on the mission's radio staff patterns the dramas after the popular *novelas* (soap-operas) for he
knows the pulse of his countrymen and what reaches them. However, to date much of the music and the preaching broadcast by
the missionaries is heavily colored by North American culture.

PROSPECTS FOR THE FUTURE

The pattern of church growth which began in 1962 has continued for six years (see Graph 11). The young Missionary
Church that began her distinctive denominational history in 1961
with 349 members had grown to an estimated 1750 members in 1967
(Correspondence, Elkjer 1967), thereby registering a 38 per cent
average annual growth. In 1966 the Missionary Church had nineteen organized churches and sixty-four congregations located in
the three Brazilian states of Mato Grosso, Sao Paulo and Parana
(see Plate 8).

On its own initiative and with indigenous resources, the
young church has expressed its social conscience in the founding
of an orphanage in 1965, a home for unwed mothers and a rehabil-
itation center for converted prostitutes in 1966 (Correspondence
Wolff 1967).

What of the future? Missionary Orville Wolff expresses the
optimism characteristic of IMS personnel in Brazil, "A solid
base for accelerated growth has been laid during the foundation
years, and the next five years should see us pass the 5,000 member mark" (Correspondence, 1967). If it continues at its present rate of growth the IMS national church will in fact reach
the 5,000 member mark in 1971 (see Graph 12). The guarantee of
continued quality growth will be determined largely by the development of a healthy mission-church relationship and of an
informed church growth perspective. Such church growth perspective would see our principal field task as reconciling men to
to Jesus Christ, baptizing them according to the biblical in-
junction and gathering them into growing local churches. This
should not only be our principal task but also the goal against
which all field projects should be evaluated.

We have traced throughout the history of the IMS in Brazil
the persistence of the interdenominational preoccupation of its
missionaries. But now a growing concern on the part of the
missionaries for the growth of the national church has appeared.
Means are being sought by some to implement this concern. The
mission-directed Crusade at last seems to be committed to establishing churches. But the large opportunity afforded to IMS
missionaries in the South of Brazil calls for a better understanding of the ways by which the church grows and a larger

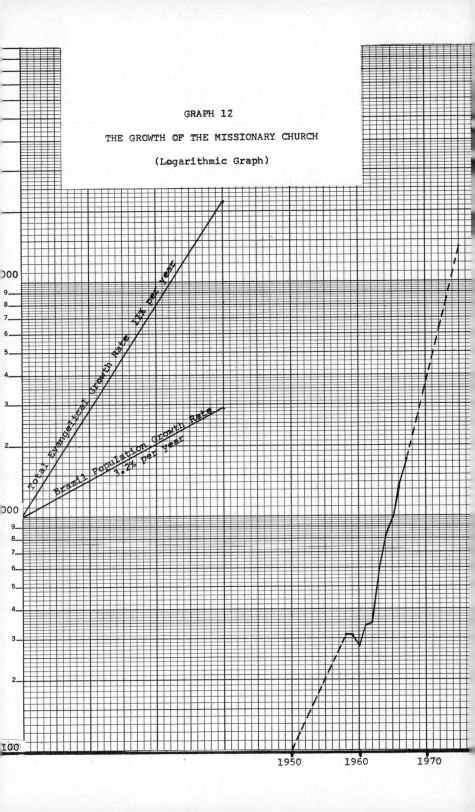

GRAPH 12

THE GROWTH OF THE MISSIONARY CHURCH

(Logarithmic Graph)

personnel involvement in the church-planting task. It is hoped
that steps will be taken to further develop the church growth
perspective among the missionaries by on-the-field seminars and
research. Furlough studies at the Fuller School of World Mission and Institute of Church Growth in Pasadena, California
should be encouraged. When the principles that underlie church
growth and the procedures that will implement it are more widely
understood and appreciated, we can expect a larger involvement
of IMS missionaries in the church-planting task.

The study of the ways the church grows should not be merely
an activity of missionary personnel. A church growth perspective can be developed among national pastors and leaders by the
dissemination of church growth literature in the indigenous
tongue. *New Patterns of Church Growth in Brazil* by William R.
Read and *Latin American Church Growth* by Read, Monterroso and
Johnson have already been published in Portuguese. Church
growth seminars for national leaders and pastors will help
create an understanding of how churches grow or what obstructs
their growth in the various sectors of the Brazilian population.

A core course should be instituted in the Bible Institute
and Seminary for prospective workers. Missionary Paul McKaughan,
a former student at the Fuller SWM-ICG serving with Overseas
Crusades, is teaching just such a course in the Free Methodist
Seminary in Sao Paulo.

Later, planning conferences with both missionaries and nationals participating could be held in which both a working plan
of co-operation, and an overall strategy for the field could be
formulated--all of this leading toward the fulfillment of the
task of planting churches as a goal shared by missionary and
nationals alike. Such a church growth understanding on the part
of national pastors and leaders coupled with the new commitment
of IMS missionaries to plant and develop growing local churches
will enable the national church to experience its greatest
growth potential.

Many problems and possibilities remain to be researched in
order to find creative new solutions. Four areas demanding im-
mediate serious investigation are: 1) studying Brazil's devel-
opmental progress and plans in order to identify those receptive
areas of the country where growing local churches should be
started, 2) locating and training indigenous leaders, 3) mobilizing the lay witness in established as well as new churches
and 4) analysing the mission budget to determine how present
expenditures are helping the national church realize its growth
potential and planning future expenditures for greater church
growth dividends.

PLATE 9

MISSION—NATIONAL CHURCH RELATIONSHIP AND MINISTRIES

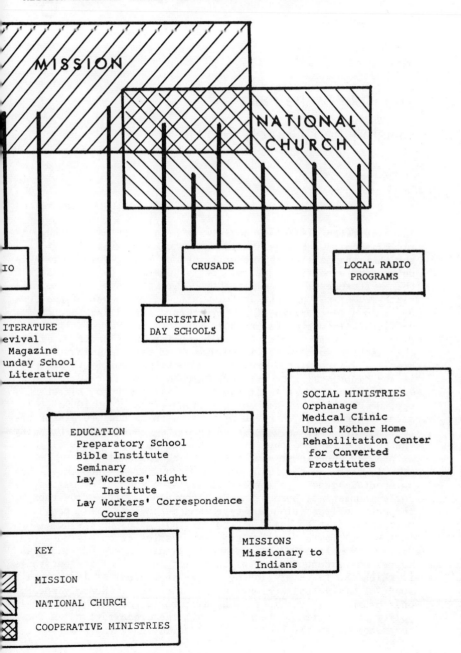

6

The Role of the Faith
Mission and Church Growth

THE UNIQUE FITNESS OF THE FAITH MISSION FOR CHURCH PLANTING

The faith missionary has always been known as an evangelistic missionary. Evangelism is his watchword. This is not to say that the passion to reconcile men to God by Jesus Christ is unique to faith missionaries, but is generally characteristic of them. Because of his commitment to Christ's commission to disciple men of all nations and his faith in the power of the Gospel unto salvation, the faith missionary is willing to endure difficult circumstances and work for long periods of time among even a resistant people. He is known for his pioneer spirit. This is borne out by the large number of faith missionaries in Brazil (175) committed exclusively to tribal work. To some he is the "ideal" missionary. Dr. Ralph Winter has said, "Though we may in some cases fault the faith missionary for his strategy, we cannot doubt his consecration" (Interview, 1969a). It seems logical that when the faith missionary adds to his urgency to find the lost, an understanding of the necessity of bringing the found ones into the Father's house, he will be equally concerned for the ministry of establishing churches.

Furthermore the faith mission enjoys great autonomy. The horizontal agency, in matters of decision and policy making, is for all practical purposes a self-contained unit. True enough, the doctrinal position and types and methods of field ministry must commend it to the constituency that makes up its home-support base. Faith missions and missionaries certainly must "sell" themselves in their promotional ministry. But there is no person (except God) or organization outside of its own ranks to which the faith mission must give an account of its use of funds or its actual achievements on the field. Humanly speaking only promotional considerations dictate to the faith mission its policy and practice. Perhaps of all the organizational structures common to the ecclesiastical world, only the Roman

Catholic orders show the same degree of freedom and autonomy, and even they make nominal reports to Rome. It is interesting to note that the orders evolved their particular structure to fulfill the apostolic ministry of the church and the Protestant faith missions developed along the same lines for the same purpose (Winter 1969:05,04).

It is also true that the freedom enjoyed by the faith mission may particularly suit the need of the church planter who wants to plant churches whose forms of worship and even church government will be in harmony with indigenous cultural patterns. Thus the Baptist, Methodist and Presbyterian workers are committed to planting Baptist, Methodist and Presbyterian churches while the faith missionary is potentially free to be far more relevant culturally.

Although the essential structure of the faith mission seems uniquely suited to the apostolic task of founding vital, growing and culturally relevant Christian churches and is not inherently anti-denominational, the faith missionary may on the other hand be gravely deficient in this respect. Because of the anti-denominational spirit in which many have been trained, there is a general tendency among faith missionaries to play down the importance of the church as a visible local assembly of believers. In all such cases he tends to ignore or disparage the various forms of government and organization that have developed in the traditional churches. Concern for church polity and evangelism tend to be viewed as mutually exclusive by the faith missionary. But he could be and should be a zealous student of ecclesiastical forms and do his best to understand the workings of every denominational and independent church available to his scrutiny. Even if the church he plants overseas takes on a totally new organizational structure, his knowledge of existing structures will serve as the background for the innovated structures devised along with national Christians to fit the new cultural context.

The faith missionary who is a church planter will thus also need to be a student of cultures. He should be aware of many cultures and give special attention to the particular culture of the people among whom he works. He will need to know how his people make decisions--individually or by group consensus. He will want to know the leadership patterns of the people and the family relationships through which the Gospel may potentially travel. He will need to know the culture well enough to distinguish what is so thoroughly pagan in the lives of the people as to require a Christian functional substitute.

The faith missionary as church planter may have to develop a new doctrinal latitude. If he has forged his biblical doctrine in the fires of the liberal-fundamentalist controversy, then he must recognize the particular polemical emphasis in his own cultural heritage. Hopefully he will maintain his doctrine based squarely on the authoritative Scriptures but with a happy expectancy of new insight and understanding through his national brethren as they, too, are taught by the Scriptures and the Holy Spirit. The rigid requirement of conformity to an imported doctrinal position can be a subtle form of paternalism and missionary dominance.

The faith missionary as church planter should also have a deep sense of apostleship. He should be convinced that Christ wants him to found new churches and to extend the Gospel. He needs to believe that his modern ministry is in direct succession with the great apostles of the New Testament. And like them he believes that men can lay no other foundation than that which is already laid which is Jesus Christ. He is not merely an overseas church worker but a missionary--a twentieth century apostle of Jesus Christ.

NEEDED -- TWO NEW FAITH MISSION AGENCIES

After examining many small agencies producing little results, and after finding some duplications, it must be wondered how we could recommend two new faith mission agencies. This suggestion certainly is not derived from any desire to see the proliferation of agencies but from a recognition of two real needs not met by existing missions.

In the first place we need a research agency that can evaluate all others. As was mentioned above, the faith mission agency tends to give account to no one. In some cases these agencies even encourage their missionaries to keep "family secrets" and not to "hang out the dirty linen." Thus an independent agency is necessary to evaluate the many factors that a mission cannot satisfactorily assess from within. We know very little of the way most agencies spend funds or what results on the field from these expenditures. For example, two faith mission agencies each receive from their supporters roughly 200,000 dollars per year. One agency has four missionaries on the foreign field and the other has forty. The agency with only four missionaries spends the major part of its income in the United States on a radio broadcast. There is a crying need for an independent faith mission agency that would evaluate sympathetically and realistically the field results, mission expenditures and policies of all other agencies: a combination of Dun and Bradstreet and Consumers' Research for Christian investors.

The second agency that is needed is a service church planter. As more and more faith missions turn to the church-planting task, new denominations will result. In some areas of the world this will result in an unhealthly proliferation. In view of this problem, the Worldwide Evangelization Crusade has done some creative thinking. The WEC policy relating to churches founded by its missionaries in Brazil is that when a church becomes "adult" and self-supporting, it will make a choice between two options: 1) to be an independent Evangelical church or 2) to join an existing denomination (Correspondence, 1969). Another approach to the problem is the example of the China Inland Mission (now Overseas Missionary Fellowship). That group established different areas in which, respectively, they set up churches after the Anglican, Baptist and Presbyterian order of worship and government. The intention was for those CIM churches later to be incorporated into their kindred denominations (Latourette 1944:329 and Taylor 1943:416).

The mission we here suggest would be an agency similar to the Overseas Crusades which we examined in Chapter 4. It would be a service mission and the service rendered would be to plant churches and turn them over to the national denominations.

THE EMERGENCE OF GREATER CO-OPERATION BETWEEN THE HORIZONTAL AND VERTICAL AGENCIES

Tragically, the suspicion between the faith missions and the denominations seems to be mutual. Some faith missions view the denominations as suspect in regard to doctrinal correctness. This is particularily true of those agencies that arose after 1938 (Lindsell 1962:195). The denominations sometimes suspect the faith missions of carrying off monies that belong to their own denominational mission boards.

Yet there have been some recent examples of co-operation between faith agencies and the denominations. A small newly emerging denomination has at times adopted a faith mission of its own doctrinal persuasion as its "mission board." Such was the case with the Evangelical Methodist Church which adopted both the Oriental Missionary Society and the World Gospel Mission as its official "mission boards." Many times a denominational agency and a faith mission agency (even a church-planting faith mission), will both co-operate with the same national church on the field. Also, of course, local denominational churches often support missionaries serving with faith missions.

Beyond these instances of token co-operation, there appears to be a new thing on the horizon. Though no larger than Elijah's cloud, it may yet prove to be an outpouring of blessing on the modern missionary movement. The indicator that there is emerging a new co-operation between the horizontal and vertical agencies is the rise in the United States of a group of faith missions around 1948 with a different attitude towards the traditional denominations. Some have classified these agencies theologically as neo-evangelicals. Our concern, however, is not with their theology per se but with their philosophy of mission and their attitudes toward the traditional denominations. Three agencies that would be characteristic of this group are The Billy Graham Evangelistic Association, World Vision International and Overseas Crusades.

The attitude of these agencies concerning the traditional denominations is non-hostile. Their philosophy of mission is aid to the denominations--especially assistance in evangelism. The many pastors' conferences conducted by World Vision International all over the world would be one example. The 1969 Minneapolis U. S. Congress on Evangelism is another example. Here a horizontal agency, The Billy Graham Evangelistic Association, assisted by personnel from other horizontal agencies, contributed very strategically to a congress that brought together ninety denominations. It is impossible to predict at this time how far the overtures of aid made by these horizontal groups will go to bring the faith missions and denominations into a place of new understanding and mutual respect, but we dare hope for still more effective co-operation in the continuing apostolic task that Christ has given to His Church.

APPENDIX

A   DIRECTORY OF FOREIGN MISSION AGENCIES AT WORK IN BRAZIL

B   BRAZIL MISSIONARY PERSONNEL DEPLOYMENT QUESTIONNAIRE

APPENDIX A

DIRECTORY OF FOREIGN MISSION AGENCIES AT WORK IN BRAZIL

This is an alphabetical listing of the foreign agencies currently working in Brazil according to their organizational names and home base addresses. Where available, the Brazilian name by which the organization is known follows. Where available, dates of entrance into the country of the mission agencies are given.

1. ACRE GOSPEL MISSION, Cruzada de Evangelizacao do Acre e Amazonas, 13 Willowbank Drive, Belfast 6, North Ireland, 1934.

2. AGRICULTURAL MISSIONS, 475 Riverside Drive, New York, New York 10027.

3. AIR MAIL FROM GOD MISSION (Now called Trans-World Missions), 4205 Santa Monica Boulevard, Los Angeles, California 90029, 1965.

4. ALLIAN-MISSION-BARMEN, Missao Evangelica Independente do Brasil, 56 Wuppertal - Vohwinkel, Falkenhaynstr. 11, Germany, 1955.

5. AMAZON MISSION, Missao Amazonas, P.O. Box 304, Gary, Indiana 46406, 1950.

6. AMERICAN LUTHERAN CHURCH, Missao Evangelica Luterana, Division of World Missions, 422 S. Fifth Street, Minneapolis, Minnesota 55415, 1953.

7. ANGLICAN EPISCOPAL CHURCH, The Church of England, London, England.

8. APOSTOLIC CHRISTIAN CHURCH, Apostolic Christian Church Foundation, P.O. Box 5233, Akron, Ohio 44313, 1962.

9. APOSTOLIC CHRISTIAN CHURCH IN THE U.S., Corporacao Igreja Nazareno, Francesville, Indiana 47946, 1915.

10, APOSTOLIC CHURCH OF OKLAHOMA, Instituto Apostolico do Brasil, Box 9155, Tulsa, Oklahoma.

11. ARMENIAN MISSIONARY SOCIETY OF AMERICA, 156 Fifth Avenue, New York, New York 10010, 1960.

12. ASSEMBLIES OF GOD, GENERAL COUNCIL, Conselho Geral das
     Assembleias de Deus, 1445 Boonville Avenue, Spring-
     field, Missouri 65802, 1935.

13. ASSOCIATION FOR CHRISTIAN LITERATURE, Box 2141, Dallas,
     Texas 75221, 1961.

14. ASSOCIATION OF BAPTISTS FOR WORLD EVANGELISM, Associacao
     dos Batistas Evangelismo Mundial, 1304 Schaff Building,
     1505 Race Street, Philadelphia, Pennsylvania 19102,
     1942.

15. BAPTIST BIBLE FELLOWSHIP INTERNATIONAL, Missao Batista Bib-
     lica do Brasil, P.O. Box 106, Springfield, Missouri
     65801.

16. BAPTIST FAITH MISSIONS, 975 E. Grand Blvd., Detroit, Mich-
     igan 48207.

17. BAPTIST GENERAL CONFERENCE, Uniao Batista Evangelica,
     Board of Foreign Missions, 5750 North Ashland Avenue,
     Chicago, Illinois 60626, 1957.

18. BAPTIST INTERNATIONAL MISSIONS, P.O. Box 696, Rossville,
     Georgia 30741.

19. BAPTIST MID-MISSIONS, Sociedade Evangelizadora, 4205 Ches-
     ter Avenue, Cleveland, Ohio 44103, 1936.

20. BAPTIST MISSIONARY SOCIETY, 93 Gloucester Place, London,
     W.1., England, 1953.

21. BEREAN MISSION, 3536 Russell Boulevard, St. Louis, Mis-
     souri 63104, 1967.

22. BETHANY FELLOWSHIP, Betania do Brasil, 6820 Auto Club Road,
     Minneapolis, Minnesota 55420, 1957.

23. BETHANY MISSIONARY ASSOCIATION, Sociedade Betania, 2201
     East Sixth Street, Long Beach, California 90814.

24. BETHSEDA MISSIONS, Missao Betseda do Brasil, 2950 Metro
     Drive, Minneapolis, Minnesota 55420, 1957.

25. BIBLE CONFERENCES AND MISSIONS, Sociedade Biblica Filadel-
     fia, Reeves, Louisiana 70658, 1963.

26. BIBLE LITERATURE INTERNATIONAL, P.O. Box 477, Columbus,
     Ohio 43216.

27. BIBLE MEMORY ASSOCIATION INTERNATIONAL, Memorizadores da
    Biblia Internacional, Box 12000 Wellston Station, St.
    Louis, Missouri 63112, 1965.

28. BILLY GRAHAM EVANGELISTIC ASSOCIATION, Associacao Billy
    Graham, 1300 Harmon Place, Minneapolis, Minnesota
    55403.

29. BRAZIL CHRISTIAN MISSION, Missao Crista do Brasil, 1664
    Poplar, Denver, Colorado 80220, 1948.

30. BRAZIL EVANGELISTIC MISSION, Missao Evangelistica Brasi-
    leira, 7 Greenwood Avenue, Laverstock, Salisbury, Wilts,
    England, 1963.

31. BRAZIL GOSPEL FELLOWSHIP MISSION, Sociedade Evangelizadora,
    319 West Reynolds, Springfield, Illinois 62702, 1939.

32. BRAZIL INLAND MISSION, 2507 West Malone Avenue, Peoria,
    Illinois 61605, 1954.

33. BRAZIL MISSION (Church of Christ), P.O. Box 424, Glendora,
    California 91740.

34. BRAZIL MISSION WITHIN THE GERMAN FELLOWSHIP DEACONRY, 335
    Marbury (Lahn), Friedrich - Naumann - Str. 15, Germany,
    1932.

35. BRAZILIAN BIBLE MISSION, 34 East Esk Road, Newport, Mon.,
    England.

36. BRETHREN CHURCH, NATIONAL FELLOWSHIP (Grace Brethren),
    Missao da Igreja dos Irmaos, P.O. Box 588, Winona Lake,
    Indiana 46590, 1949.

37. CAMPUS CRUSADE, Arrowhead Springs, San Bernardino, Califor-
    nia 92403, 1968.

38. CHILD EVANGELISM FELLOWSHIP, INTERNATIONAL, Alianca Pro-
    Evangelizacao das Criancas, P.O. Box 1156, Grand Ra-
    pids, Michigan 49501, 1942.

39. CHRISTIAN AND MISSIONARY ALLIANCE, Alianca Crista e Mis-
    sionaria, 260 W. 44th Street, New York, New York 10036,
    1962.

40. CHRISTIAN BIBLE MISSION, 873 Scott Street, Muskegon, Mich-
    igan, 1965.

41. CHRISTIAN CHILDREN'S FUND, 108 South Third, Richmond, Vir-
    ginia 23204, 1965.

42. CHRISTIAN CHURCH WORLD MISSIONS (Disciples of Christ), 205
East Main Street, Enterprise, Oregon 97828.

43. CHRISTIAN LIFE MISSIONS , P.O. Box 824, Wheaton, Illinois
60187, 1964.

44. CHRISTIAN LITERATURE CRUSADE , Cruzada de Literatura Evangelica do Brasil, 701 Pennsylvania Avenue, Box 51,
Fort Washington, Pennsylvania 19034, 1958.

45. CHRISTIAN MISSIONARY FELLOWSHIP , Comunidade Crista Missio-
nario do Brasil, P.O. Box 26306, Lawrence, Indiana
46226, 1957.

46. CHRISTIAN MISSIONS IN MANY LANDS (Plymouth Brethren), 16
Hudson Street, New York, New York 10013, 1896.

47. CHRISTIAN REFORMED CHURCH, Board of Foreign Missions, 2850
Kalamazoo Avenue, S. E., Grand Rapids, Michigan 49508,
1934.

48. CHURCH OF GOD Missionary Board, Box 2498, Anderson, Indiana 46011, 1969.

49. CHURCH OF GOD World Missions Board, Igreja de Deus do Brasil, 1080 Montogomery Avenue, Cleveland, Tennessee
37312.

50. CHURCH OF GOD OF PROPHECY , World Mission Committee, Bible
Place, Cleveland, Tennessee 37311, 1965.

51. CHURCH OF THE NAZARENE , Igreja do Nazareno, Department of
Foreign Missions, 6401 The Paseo, Kansas City, Missouri
64131, 1958.

52. CHURCH WORLD SERVICE , 475 Riverside Drive, New York, New
York 10027, 1954.

53. CLEVELAND HEBREW MISSION , Sociedade Brasileira Amigos de
Israel, P.O. Box 18056, Cleveland Heights, Ohio 44118.

54. CO-LABORERS, 3027 Queen Avenue, North, Minneapolis, Minnesota 55411, 1955.

55. COLONIA EVANGELICA ACAILANDIA, Route 4 Box 232, Goshen,
Indiana 46526.

56. CONSERVATIVE BAPTIST FOREIGN MISSIONARY SOCIETY , Missao
Batista Conservadora, P.O. Box 5, Wheaton, Illinois
60187, 1945.

57. DEUTSCHE INDIANER PIONIER MISSION, Stuttgart-Gerlingen,
     Ganswiesenweg 37, Germany, 1962.

58. DUTCH EVANGELICAL REFORMED CHURCH MISSION, Missao do Igreja
     Evangelica Reformada do Brasil, Reformed Churches in
     the Netherlands, Wilhelminalaam 3, Baarn, Holland, 1960.

59. DUTCH PENTECOSTAL MISSIONS, Missionaria Evangelica Pente-
     costal, Rhoden 17, Steenbergen, Holland.

60. ELIM MISSIONARY SOCIETY, Igreja Pentecostal Elim, 20 Clar-
     ence Avenue, Clapham Park, London, W. W. 4, England,
     1962.

61. ESCOLE BIBLIQUE, Acao Biblica do Brasil, Le Roc, Cologny,
     Geneve, Suica.

62. EVANGELICAL ENTERPRISES, Empresas Evangelicas, P.O. Box
     1555, Topeka, Kansas 66601, 1959.

63. EVANGELICAL LUTHERAN CHURCH OF CANADA, Board of World Mis-
     sions, 212 Wiggins Avenue, Saskatoo, Saskatchewan,
     Canada, 1958.

64. (EVANGELICAL) MENNONITE CHURCH, Associacao Evangelica Men-
     onita, Board of Missions and Charities, P.O. Box 370,
     Elkhart, Indiana 46514, 1954.

65. EVANGELICAL UNION OF SOUTH AMERICA, Uniao Evangelica Sul-
     Americana, 78 W. Hudson Avenue, Englewood, New Jersey
     07631, 1931.

66. EVANGELICAL UNITED BRETHREN CHURCH (Now part of United
     Methodist Church), The Board of Missions, 601 West
     Riverview Avenue, Dayton, Ohio 45406, 1948.

67. FELLOWSHIP OF INDEPENDENT MISSIONS, P.O. Box 72, Fairless
     Hills, Pennsylvania 19030.

68. FREE METHODIST CHURCH OF NORTH AMERICA, Winona Lake, Indi-
     ana 46590, 1936.

69. FREE WILL BAPTISTS, NATIONAL ASSOCIATION, Missao Batista
     Livre do Brasil, 1134 Murfreesboro Road, Nashville,
     Tennessee 37202, 1958.

70. GARR MEMORIAL CHURCH, 200 Tuchaseegee Road, Charlotte,
     North Carolina 28201.

71. GNADAUER BRAZILIAN MISSION, Sociedade Uniao Crista, 7306
        Denkendorf, Dreis Esslingen a.M., Locherhaldenstrasse
        20, Germany, 1927.

72. GO-YE FELLOWSHIP, P.O. Box 26193, Los Angeles, California
        90026, 1956.

73. GOSPEL FELLOWSHIP MISSIONS, Bob Jones University, Green-
        ville, South Carolina 29614.

74. GOSPEL LIGHT PUBLICATIONS (GLINT), Edicoes Luz do Evangelho,
        725 East Colorado Boulevard, Glendale, California
        91205.

75. GOSPEL OF JESUS CHURCH (Iesu Fukuin Kyddan), 1548 Shimohoya,
        Tanshi P.O., Tokyo-to, Japan, 1960.

76. HEBREW EVANGELIZATION SOCIETY, Esperanca de Israel, P.O.
        Box 707, Los Angeles, California 90053.

77. HOSPITAL CHRISTIAN FELLOWSHIP, Uniao do Pessoal Medico e
        Hospitalar Cristao, P.O. Box 353, Kempton Park, Trans-
        val, South Africa.

78. INDEPENDENT BIBLE BAPTIST MISSIONS, P.O. Box 48, Englewood,
        Colorado 80110, 1957.

79. INDEPENDENT FAITH MISSION, Voz Biblica Brasileira, 3346 E.
        M. 36, Pinckney, Michigan 48169, 1965.

80. INTER-AMERICAN EVANGELISTIC ASSOCIATION, 2201 East Sixth
        Street, Long Beach, California 90814.

81. INTER-AMERICAN MISSIONARY SOCIETY, Sociedade Missionaria
        Inter-Americana, The Oriental Missionary Society, Box
        A, Greenwood, Indiana 46142, 1950.

82. INTERNATIONAL BOARD OF JEWISH MISSIONS, P.O. Box 1256, At-
        lanta, Georgia 30301.

83. INTERNATIONAL CHURCH OF THE FOURSQUARE GOSPEL, Igreja do
        Evangelho Quadrangular, 1100 Glendale Boulevard, Los
        Angeles, California 90026, 1945.

84. INTERNATIONAL COMMITTEE OF YMCA'S OF U.S. AND CANADA, 291
        Broadway, New York, New York 10007, 1893.

85. INTERNATIONAL FELLOWSHIP OF EVANGELICAL STUDENTS, Alianca
        Biblica Universitaria do Brasil, 436 Rowell Boulevard,
        Fresno, California 93721, 1957.

86. JAPAN ALLIANCE CHURCH, 255 Itsukaichi-Machi, Saeki Gun, Hiroshima Ken, Japan, 1959.

87. JAPAN BAPTIST CONVENTION, Batista do Japao, 2-350 Nishio-kubo, Shinjuku-ku, Tokyo, Japan, 1964.

88. JAPAN EVANGELICAL LUTHERAN CHURCH, 303-3 Hyakunin-cho, Shinjuku-ku, Tokyo, Japan, 1964.

89. JAPAN HOLINESS CHURCH, Megurita, Higashimurayama-Shi, Tokyo, Japan, 1925.

90. JAPANESE EVANGELICAL MISSIONARY SOCIETY, 112 North San Pedro Street, Los Angeles, California 90012, 1964.

91. KIRCHICHES AUSSENAMT DER EVANGELISCHEN, Igreja Evangelica da Confissao Luterana do Brasil, 6 Frankfurt, Main, Postfach 4025, Germany.

92. LAUBACH LITERACY, P.O. Box 131, Syracuse, New York 13210.

93. LAYMEN'S OVERSEAS SERVICE, P.O. Box 5031, Jackson, Mississippi 39216.

94. LEIPZIG EVANGELICAL LUTHERAN MISSION, Paul-List-Str. 17/19, 701 Leipzig, 1, Germany, 1955.

95. LESTER SUMRALL EVANGELISTIC ASSOCIATION, P.O. Box 12, 19440 Ireland Road, South Bend, Indiana 46624, 1966.

96. LIFE MISSION, R.D. 1, Perkiomenville, Pennsylvania 18074, 1965.

97. LITERATURE CRUSADES, P.O. Box 203, Prospect Heights, Illinois 60070, 1968.

98. LUTHERAN CHURCH - MISSOURI SYNOD, Igreja Evangelica Luterana do Brasil, Board of Missions, 210 North Broadway, St. Louis, Missouri 63102, 1899.

99. LUTHERAN WORLD FEDERATION, 315 Park Avenue South, New York, New York 10010.

100. LUTHERAN WORLD RELIEF, 315 Park Avenue South, New York, New York 10010, 1948.

101. MARBERGER MISSION, Igreja de Christianismo Decidido, Marburg Hahn, Stressemannstr 22, Postfoch 600 P.A. 2, Germany, 1932.

102. MENNONITE BRETHREN CHURCHES, GENERAL CONFERENCE, Missao
     Irmaos Menonitas, Board of Missions and Services, 315
     Lincoln, Hillsboro, Kansas 67063, 1944.

103. MENNONITE CENTRAL COMMITTEE, 21 South 12th Street, Akron,
     Pennsylvania 17501, 1964.

104. MENNONITE CHURCH, GENERAL CONFERENCE, Board of Missions,
     P.O. Box 347, Newton, Kansas 67114, 1958.

105. UNITED METHODIST CHURCH, World Division, Board of Missions,
     475 Riverside Drive, New York, New York 10027, 1880.

106. METHODISTEN-KIRCHE IN DEUTCHLAND, Junta de Missoes da Igre-
     ja Metodista do Brasil, 6 Frank-Main-Ginhein, Ginn-
     heimer-Landstr. 174, Alemanha.

107. MISSION TO AMAZONIA (Merged with Evangelical Union of
     South America), P.O. Box 1145, Brookings, Oregon
     97415, 1952.

108. MISSIONARY AND SOUL WINNING FELLOWSHIP, Alianca Missio-
     naria do Brasil, P.O. Box 7271, Long Beach, California
     90807, 1955.

109. MISSIONARY AVIATION FELLOWSHIP, Asas de Socorro, P.O. Box
     2828, Fullerton, California, 1955.

110. MISSIONARY CENTRE OF THE REFORMED CHURCHES IN THE NETHER-
     LANDS, Wilhelminalaan 3, Baarn, Netherlands, 1958.

111. MISSIONSWERK MITTERNACHTSRUF, Obra Missionaria Brado da
     Meia Noite, Postfach 150, 8034, Zurich, Schweiz.

112. NATIONAL ASSOCIATION OF CONGREGATIONAL CHRISTIAN CHURCHES,
     176 W. Wisconsin Avenue, Milwaukee, Wisconsin.

113. NAVIGATORS, P.O. Box 1659, Colorado Springs, Colorado
     80901, 1963.

114. NEW TESTAMENT MISSIONARY UNION, Missao Neotestamentaria,
     256 Oak Street, Audubon, New Jersey 18106.

115. NEW TRIBES MISSION, Missao Novas Tribos do Brasil, Wood-
     worth, Wisconsin 53194, 1949.

116. NORTH AMERICAN BAPTISTS ASSOCIATION, Associacao Batista
     Norte-Americana, 716 Main Street, LIttle Rock, Arkan-
     sas 72201, 1950.

117. NORTH AMERICAN BAPTIST GENERAL MISSIONARY SOCIETY, 7308
      Madison Street, Forest Park, Illinois 60130, 1966.

118. OREBRO MISSIONEN (Swedish Baptists), Sociedade Missionaria
      Batista Independente, Box 330, Orebro, Sweden, 1912.

119. OVERSEAS CRUSADES, Servico de Evangelizacao Para a America
      Latina (SEPAL), 265 Lytton Avenue, Palo Alto, Califor-
      nia 94301, 1963.

120. PENIEL CHAPEL MISSIONARY SOCIETY, Sociedade Missionaria de
      Peniel, Kensington Park Road, North Kensington, London
      W 11, England, 1932.

121. PENTECOSTAL ASSEMBLIES OF CANADA, Overseas Missions De-
      partment, 10 Overlea Boulevard, Toronto 17, Ontario,
      Canada, 1963.

122. PENTECOSTAL CHURCH OF CHRIST, Igreja de Cristo Pentecostal,
      P.O. Box 263, London, Ohio 43140, 1935.

123. PENTECOSTAL CHURCH OF GOD OF AMERICA, Igreja de Deus Pente-
      costal do Brasil, Missions Board, P.O. Box 816, Joplin,
      Missouri 64802, 1956.

124. PILGRIM FELLOWSHIP, Ministerio Evangelico do Brasil, 1201
      Chestnut Street, Philadelphia, Pennsylvania 19107, 1948.

125. PILGRIM HOLINESS CHURCH (The Wesleyan Church), 230 E. Ohio
      Street, Indianapolis, Indiana 46204, 1960.

126. POCKET TESTAMENT LEAGUE, Aliga do Testamento do Bolso,
      49 Honeck Street, Englewood, New Jersey 07631, 1966.

127. PRESBYTERIAN CHURCH IN THE U.S., Missao Presbiteriana do
      Brasil, Board of World Missions, P.O. Box 330, Nash-
      ville, Tennessee 37202, 1869.

128. PRESBYTERIAN FOREIGN MISSIONS, INDEPENDENT BOARD, Igreja
      Presbiteriana Conservadora, 246 West Walnut Lane, Phil-
      adelphia, Pennsylvania 19144, 1946.

129. PROTESTANT EPISCOPAL CHURCH IN U.S.A., Igreja Episcopal do
      Brasil, Domestic and Foreign Mission Society, 815
      Second Avenue, New York, New York 10017, 1907.

130. SALVATION ARMY, Exercito de Salvacao, 122 W. 14th Street,
      New York, New York 10011, 1922.

131. SCRIPTURE UNION, 239 Fairfield, Upper Darby, Pennsylvania
      19082.

132. SEVENTH-DAY ADVENTISTS, Adventistas de Setimo Dia, 6840
Eastern Avenue, N.W., Tacoma Park, Washington, D.C.
20012, 1895.

133. SLAVIC GOSPEL ASSOCIATION, 2434 North Kedzie Boulevard,
Chicago, Illinois 60647, 1950.

134. SOCIETY FOR DISTRIBUTING THE HOLY SCRIPTURES TO THE JEWS,
237 Shaftesbury AVenue, London, W.C. 2, England.

135. SOUTH AMERICAN AND WORLD MISSION, 412 Laura Lee Avenue,
Tallahassee, Florida 32301, 1963.

136. SOUTH AMERICAN INDIAN MISSION, P.O. Box 769, Lake Worth,
Florida 33460, 1914.

137. SOUTHERN BAPTIST CONVENTION, Missao Batista Equatorial do
Brasil, Foreign Mission Board, P.O. Box 6597, Richmond,
Virginia 23230, 1965.

138. SOUTHERN CROSS SCRIPTURE MISSION, 3030 Old Decatur Road,
Apartment 303B, Atlanta, Georgia 30305, 1965.

139. SPANISH AMERICAN INLAND MISSION, Cruzada Interamericana do
Brasil, P.O. Box 782, Joplin, Missouri 64802, 1962.

140. SWEDISH BAPTIST UNION OF FINLAND, Radhusgat. 44, Vasa,
Finland.

141. SWEDISH FREE MISSION (Svenska Fria Missionen - Assembleia
de Deus), Filadelfiaforsamlingen, Rorstrandsgatan 5,
Stockholm 6, Sweden, 1910.

142. THINGS TO COME MISSION, P.O. Box 96, Cope, Colorado 80812,
1969.

143. UNEVANGELIZED FIELDS MISSION, Missao Crista Evangelica do
Brasil, P.O. Box 306, Bala-Cynwyd, Pennsylvania 19004,
1931.

144. UNITED CHURCH OF CANADA, Junta de Missoes da Igreja Meto-
dista do Brasil, Board of World Mission, 85 St. Clair
Avenue, East, Toronto 7, Ontario, Canada, 1961.

145. UNITED CHURCH OF CHRIST, Igreja Evangelica Congregacional
do Brasil, Board for World Ministries, 475 Riverside
Drive, New York, New York, 1962.

146. UNITED MISSIONARY FELLOWSHIP, Acampamento Biblico Pioneiro,
P.O. Box 214622, Sacramento, California 95821, 1948.

147. UNITED MISSIONARY SOCIETY, Sociedade Missionaria Unida do
     Brasil, The Missionary Church, 3901 South Wayne Avenue,
     Fort Wayne, Indiana 46807, 1955.

148. UNITED MISSIONS, Alexander City, Alabama 35010.

149. UNITED PENTECOSTAL CHURCH, Igreja Pentecostal Unida do
     Brasil, Foreign Missionary Department, 3645 South
     Grand Boulevard, St. Louis, Missouri 63118.

150. UNITED PRESBYTERIAN CHURCH IN THE U.S.A., Missao Presbi-
     teriana do Brasil Central, Commission on Ecumenical
     Mission and Relations, 475 Riverside Drive, 9th Floor,
     New York, New York 10027, 1859.

151. UNITED WORLD MISSION, P.O. Box 8000, St. Petersburg, Flor-
     ida 33738, 1961.

152. WEST AMAZON MISSION, Missao da Amazonia Ocidental, 18 Mar-
     tens Close, Shrivenham, Berkshire, England, 1953.

153. WEST INDIES MISSION, Missao Pan-Americana, Route 1, Box
     279, Homer City, Pennsylvania 15748, 1957.

154. WORD OF LIFE FELLOWSHIP, Palavra da Vida, 91 Main Street,
     Orange, New Jersey 17050, 1958.

155. WORLD BAPTIST FELLOWSHIP MISSION AGENCY, 3001 West Divi-
     sion, Arlington, Texas 76010, 1961.

156. WORLD COUNCIL OF CHURCHES, Commission on World Mission and
     Evangelism, 475 Riverside Drive, Room 439, New York,
     New York 10027.

157. WORLD GOSPEL CRUSADES, P.O. Box 3, Upland, California
     91786, 1955.

158. WORLD GOSPEL MISSION, P.O. Box 948, Marion, Indiana 46592.

159. WORLD GOSPEL MISSIONARY SOCIETY, (Sekai Fukuin Senkyo Kai),
     c/o Box 5, Ibarake, Osaku Fu, Japan, 1965.

160. WORLD LITERATURE CRUSADE, Box 1313, Studio City, Califor-
     nia 91604.

161. WORLD MISSIONS, P.O. Box 2611, Long Beach, California
     10001, 1964.

162. WORLD MISSIONS TO CHILDREN, Missoes Mundiais para Crian-
     cas, P.O. Box 1048, Grants Pass, Oregon 97526, 1957.

163. WORLD RADIO MISSIONARY FELLOWSHIP, Voz dos Andes, P.O. Box
     691, Miami, Florida 33147, 1963.

164. WORLD VISION INTERNATIONAL, P.O. Box 0, Pasadena, Califor-
     nia 91101.

165. WORLD WIDE MISSIONS, P.O. Box G, Pasadena, California
     91109, 1963.

166. WORLDWIDE EVANGELIZATION CRUSADE, Missao de Evangelizacao
     Mundial, P.O. Box A, Fort Washington, Pennsylvania
     19034, 1957.

167. WYCLIFFE BIBLE TRANSLATORS , P.O. Box 1960, Santa Ana,
     California 92702, 1956.

168. YOUNG LIFE CAMPAIGN, Alvo da Mocidade, P.O. Box 520, Col-
     orado Springs, Colorado 80901, 1963.

169. YOUTH FOR CHRIST INTERNATIONAL, Mocidade para Cristo, P.O.
     Box 419, Wheaton, Illinois 60187, 1950.

AGENCIES WITH ONLY BRAZIL ADDRESSES

1. AMAZON DENTAL FELLOWSHIP , Caixa Postal 302, Manaus, Amazonas.

2. ASSEMBLEIA CRISTA, Caixa Postal 5562, Sao Paulo, Sao Paulo.

3. BIBLE SOCIETY OF BRAZIL, Caixa Postal 73 e 454, Rio de
   Janeiro, Guanabara.

4. BRADO DO HORA FINAL, Caixa Postal 30.623, Sao Paulo, Sao
   Paulo.

5. BRAZIL CHRISTIAN PUBLICATIONS, (Christian Church), Caixa
   Postal 403, Goiania, Goias.

6. BRAZILIAN BAPTIST CONVENTION, Foreign Mission Board, Rua
   Senador Furtado 56, Rio de Janeiro, Guanabara.

7. BRAZILIAN EVANGELICAL CONFEDERATION, Av. Erasmo Braga 277,
   ZC-00, Rio de Janeiro, Guanabara.

8. BRAZILIAN EVANGELISTIC ASSOCIATION, Caixa Postal 19.010,
   Sao Paulo, Sao Paulo.

9. BRETHREN ASSEMBLIES (Plymouth Brethren), Rua Cel. Colares
   Moreira 523, Sao Luiz, Maranhao.

10. CHRISTIAN LITERATURE ADVANCE, Caixa Postal 2600, Sao Paulo,
     Sao Paulo.

11. CRUZADA DA NOVA VIDA, Rev. Walter Robert McAlister, Caixa
     Postal 2734, Rio de Janeiro, Guanabara.

12. IGREJA EVANGELICA SUICA, Caixa Postal 1071, ZC-07, Rio de
     Janeiro, AC-00, Guanabara.

13. IGREJA LUTERANA INDEPENDENTE, Rev. John Abel, Caixa Postal
     44, Campo Mourao, Parana.

14. IGREJA REFORMADA, Caixa Postal 171, Monte Alegre do Tele-
     maco Borba, Parana.

15. IMPRENSA DA FE, Caixa Postal 30.421, Sao Paulo, Sao Paulo.

16. INDEPENDENT PENTECOSTAL, Caixa Postal 92, Recife, Pernam-
     buco.

17. LIFE MINISTRY, Caixa Postal 30.421, Sao Paulo, Sao Paulo.

18. METROPOLITAN CHAPEL, Pastor Richard M. Shurtz, Caixa Postal
     2600, Sao Paulo, Sao Paulo.

19. MISSAO CRISTA (German Plymouth Brethren), Caixa Postal 33,
     Caceres, Mato Grosso.

20. MISSAO EVANGELICO DO INTERIOR DO BRASIL, Caixa Postal 35,
     Xanxere, Santa Catarina.

21. MISSAO MUNDO PARA CRISTO, Caixa Postal 48, Manaus, Amazonas.

22. MISSIONARY UNION FOR SOUTH AMERICA, EVANGELICAL MISSION OF,
     Caixa Postal 1738, Sao Paulo, Sao Paulo.

23. PARANA VALLEY MISSION, Guira, Parana.

24. PLYMOUTH BRETHREN, Fervedouro, Via Carangola, Minas Gerais.

25. SOCIEDADE EVANGELIZADORA DAS IGREJAS DO CRISTO, Caixa Pos-
     tal 1474, Belem, Para.

26. T. L. OSBORN EVANGELISTIC ASSOCIATION, Caixa Postal 2,
     Penha, ZC-22, Rio de Janeiro, Guanabara.

27. TESTEMUNHO BATISTA PARA ISRAEL DE SAO PAULO, Caixa Postal
     8614, Sao Paulo, Sao Paulo.

BRAZIL MISSIONARY PERSONNEL DEPLOYMENT QUESTIONNAIRE

Some mission agencies do not plant churches of their own but are devoted wholly to serving the existing missions and helping to build up existing national churches. Many other mission agencies have as their direct purpose the planting of churches and the establishment of a specific national, indigenous church. Some missions do both. It is the aim of this questionnaire to classify mission agencies in Brazil according to the degree to which they work directly in church planting or indirectly as service agencies.

1. Please indicate with a check which of the following situations corresponds most closely to yours in <u>Brazil</u>:

    _____We do not as a mission have the direct purpose of planting churches or establishing a national church.

    _____We do have this purpose of establishing a national church and

        _____are now in the process.

        _____have already founded it.

    _____We already have a national church at least in the following way(s):

        _____completely self governing

        _____completely self supporting

        _____the machinery for self propagation is completely in the <u>control</u> of the national church.

2. Give the number of paid missionary personnel in your mission on the <u>Brazil</u> field. (Include those on furlough.)

    _____Ministers

    _____Lay

3.a. Indicate how many of these missionaries are rendering a <u>voluntary</u> interdenominational service? (If you have several missionaries that give part time, tally the total. i.e., 3 missionaries give 1/3 of their time = 1 missionary).

    _____

  b. How many of your missionaries in Brazil are <u>assigned</u> to to intermission and/or interdenominational co-operative projects?

    _____

  c. How many are in direct church planting or church developing?

    _____

QUESTIONNAIRE cont.

    d. Other missionary work: _____
       (Total should equal figures given in #2)

4. Give a few examples of the type of interdenominational ser-
    vice being performed by the missionaries mentioned under
    #3a & b above of your agency in Brazil.

_____   _____   _____

5. List the Brazilian state(s) in which your missionaries are
    working:

_____

BIBLIOGRAPHY

ADAMS, Roy P.
  1968   Interview with author, May 8, 1968.

ALLEN, Roland
  1962   *Missionary Methods: St. Paul's or Ours?* Grand Rapids,
          William B. Eerdmans.

  1962a *The Spontaneous Expansion of the Church.* Grand Rapids,
          William B. Eerdmans.

AQUINO, Jonathas Thomas de
  1950   "Atheist Seeks Christ," *The Missionary Standard,* XLIX,
          11:5.

AZEVEDO, Fernando de
  1950   *Brazilian Culture: An Introduction to the Study of
          Culture in Brazil.* New York, The MacMillan Company.
          (Translated by William Rex Crawford from the original
          Portuguese.)

AZEVEDO, Thales de
  1963   *Social Change in Brazil.* Gainsville, Florida, Univer-
          sity of Florida Press.

BAER, Werner
  1965   *Industrialization and Economic Development in Brazil.*
          Homewood, Illinois, Irwin (Economic Growth Center of
          Yale University).

BARNETT, H. G.
  1953   *Innovation: The Basis of Cultural Change.* New York,
          McGraw Hill Book Company, Inc.

BARTLETT, O. R.
  1967   Letter to William R. Read, May 12, 1967.

BEAR, James Edwin
  1961   *Mission to Brazil*. Nashville, Tennessee, Board of
          World Missions, Presbyterian Church in U.S.

BELLO, Jose Maria
  1966   *A History of Modern Brazil 1889-1964*. Stanford, Cali-
          fornia, Stanford University Press. (Translated by
          James L. Taylor from the original Portuguese.)

BERG, Daniel
  n.d.   *Enviado Por Deus*. Sao Paulo, Grafica Sao Jose, S.A.

BINGLE, E. J. and GRUBB, Kenneth G., eds.
  1952   *World Christian Handbook - 1952*. London, World Domin-
          ion Press.

  1957   *World Christian Handbook - 1957*. London, World Domin-
          ion Press.

BRAGA, Erasmo
  1929   "Are Missions Wanted in Brazil?" *The Missionary Review
          of the World,* 52:611-613.

BRAGA, Erasmo and GRUBB, Kenneth G.
  1932   *The Republic of Brazil, A Survey of the Religious Sit-
          uation*. London, World Dominion Press.

BRETONES, Lauro
  n.d.   *Whirlwinds of the South, A Year of Revival in Brazil
          with Dr. J. Edwin Orr*. (Translated by Paul McKaughan
          from the original Portuguese).

CALOGEROS, Joao Candio
  1963   *A History of Brazil*. New York, Russell and Russell,
          Inc. (Translated by Perry Alvin Martin from Portu -
          guese).

CHRISTIANITY TODAY
  1969   "Mission and Missionaries 1969," Vol. XIII, 15: (April)
          20,21.

CONDE, Emilio
  1960   *Historia dos Assembleias de Deus do Brasil*. Rio de
          Janeiro, Casa Publicadora Assembleias de Deus.

CONSIDINE, John J.
  1958   *New Horizons in Latin America*. New York, Dodd, Mead,
          & Co.

CORNELL, D. L.
n.d.   Form from Worldwide Evangelization Crusade to CGRILA.

COXILL, H. Wakelin and GRUBB, Kenneth G., eds.
1962   *World Christian Handbook - 1962.* London, World Domin-
         ion Press.

1967   *World Christian Handbook - 1968.* London, Lutterworth
         Press.

DAVIS, J. Merle
1943   *How the Church Grows in Brazil.* New York, Internation-
         al Missionary Council.

DEGGAU, Arno
1967   Interview with author, June 13, 1967.

DUEWEL, Wesley
1965   Letter to William R. Read, November 24, 1965.

1966   "The Spirit's Ministry Through the Oriental Missionary
         Society." Greenwood, Indiana (Mimeographed).

1967   "Primary Doctrines Emphasized by the Oriental Mission-
         ary Society." Greenwood, Indiana (Mimeographed).

ELKJER, Charles B.
n.d.   Form from Inter-American Missionary Society to CGRILA.

1965   "Historical and Factual Questionnaire," The Oriental
         Missionary Society." Greenwood, Indiana (Mimeographed).

1967   "Musical Gems from Brazil," *The Missionary Standard,*
         LXVI, 4:2-5.

1967a   Letter to author, May 6, 1967.

ERNY, Esther
1965   "Answer to Orphans' Prayer," *The Missionary Standard,*
         LXIV, 11:17.

ERNY, Eugene A., GILLAM, William and ELKJER, Charles B.
1957   *Normas e Posicao Doutrinario da Sociedade Missionaria
         Inter-Americana no Brasil.* Londrina, Parana, Brazil.

FAUL, Donald Gene
1968   "Governing Principles of Brazilian Church Growth." An
         unpublished M.A. thesis, Department of World Missions,
         Dallas Theological Seminary.

FERREIRA, Julio Andrade
  1959   *Historia da Igreja Presbiteriana do Brasil.* Sao Paulo,
         Casa Editora Presbiteriana.

FERREIRA, Wilson
  1968   "The Presbyterian Church of Brazil - A Series of Talks."
         Unpublished term paper for Fuller School of World Mis-
         sion.

FINLEY, John F., ed.
  1926   *An Outline of Christianity.* New York, Dodd, Mead, and
         Co.

FREEDMAN, Ronald
  1964   *Population: The Vital Revolution.* New York, Double-
         day and Company.

FREYRE, Gilberto
  1963   *New World in the Tropics, The Culture of Modern Brazil.*
         New York, Random House.

FULTS, Donald L.
  1969   "Evangelism in Colombia Mobilizing the Evangelical
         Churches in 1968 and 1969." Unpublished report pre-
         pared for the Annual Convention of the EFMA, April,
         1969 (Mimeographed).

FURTADO, Celso
  1968   *The Economic Growth of Brazil.* Berkeley, California
         University of California Press. (Translated by Eric
         Charles Drysdale and Ricardo W. de Aguiar from the
         original Portuguese).

GILLAM, William
  1967   Interview with the author, April, 1967.

GINSBERG, Solomon L.
  1921   *A Missionary Adventure.* Nashville, Tennessee, Baptist
         Sunday School Board of the Southern Baptist Convention.

GODDARD, Burton L., ed.
  1967   *The Encyclopedia of Modern Christian Missions.* Camden,
         Thomas Nelson and Sons.

GRUBB, Kenneth G., ed., and BINGLE, E. J., assist. ed.
  1949   *World Christian Handbook - 1949.* London, World Domin-
         ion Press.

HAHN, Carl J.
  1950   "Brazil is Calling," *The Missionary Standard,* XLIX,
         7:12,19.

HAHN, Carl J.
  1950a *"Chegou,* Arrived," *The Missionary Standard,* XLIX, 8:9.

  1951   "What is Your IQ on Brazil?" *The Missionary Standard,*
         L, 10:5.

HAHN, Gracie
  1950b "He Leadeth Me," *The Missionary Standard,* XLIX, 9:5,17.

  1951a "Mrs. Hahn Writes," *The Missionary Standard,* L, 10:5.

  1952   "Fruit to Your Account," *The Missionary Standard,* LI,
         1:5,16.

  1952a "Gloria, Gloria, Hallelujah," *The Missionary Standard,*
         LI, 12:5,17.

HARE, Macon G.
  1969   Letter to author, Woodworth Wisconsin, May 6, 1969.

HERR, David M.
  1968   *Society and Population.* New Jersey, Prentice Hall Inc.

HERRING, Hubert
  1968   *A History of Latin America.* New York, Alfred A. Knopf.

HIRSCHMAN, Albert O.
  1965   *Journeys Toward Progress.* Garden City, New York, Dou-
         bleday and Company, Inc.

HOROWITZ, Irving
  1964   *Revolution in Brazil.* New York, E. P. Dutton & Co.,
         Inc.

HORTON, Arthur G.
  1966   *An Outline of Latin American History.* Dubuque, Iowa,
         William C. Brown Book Co.

INTER-VARSITY CHRISTIAN FELLOWSHIP
  1967   *Foreign Mission Board Directory.* Chicago, Inter-Var-
         sity Press.

JOHNSON, Harmon A.
  1968   "Research is the Key to Church Development," *Evangeli-
         cal Missions Quarterly,* (Winter) 75-88.

JOHNSON, John J.
  1958   *Political Change in Latin America: The Emergence of
         the Middle Sectors.* Stanford, California, Stanford
         University Press.

KESSLER, J. B. A.
  1967   A Study of the Older Protestant Missions and Churches
         in Peru and Chile. Goes, The Netherlands, Oosterbaan
         & le Cointre.

LAMBERT, Jacques
  1967   Latin American Social Structures and Political Insti-
         tution. Berkeley, California, University of California
         Press. (Translated by Helen Kotel.)

LASKOWSKI, W. T.
  1967   Letter to William R. Read, May 15, 1967.

LATOURETTE, Kenneth Scott
  1944   The Great Century in Northern Africa and Asia (A.D.
         1800-1914). Vol. 6 of A History of the Expansion of
         Christianity. New York, Harper and Brothers.

  1945   Advance Through the Storm. Vol. 7 of A History of the
         Expansion of Christianity. New York, Harper and Bros.

  1962   Christianity in a Revolutionary Age. New York, Harper
         and Row.

LINDSELL, Harold
  1962   "Faith Missions Since 1938," in Wilbur C. Harr (ed.),
         Frontier of the Christian World Since 1938, pp. 189-
         230.

LITERATURE CRUSADES
  1969   Letter to author, May, 1969.

MARIA DE JESUS, Carolina
  1964   Beyond All Pity. London, The New English Library
         Limited. (Translated by David St. Clair from the
         original Portuguese).

MARSHALL, Andrew
  1966   Brazil. New York, Walker and Company.

McGAVRAN, Donald A.
  1955   The Bridges of God: A Study in the Strategy of Mis-
         sions. New York, Friendship Press.

  1959   How Churches Grow. London, World Dominion Press.

McGAVRAN, Donald A., HUEGEL, John and TAYLOR, Jack
  1963   Church Growth in Mexico. Grand Rapids, William B.
         Eerdmans.

McGAVRAN, Donald A., ed.
   1965   *Church Growth and Christian Mission.* New York, Harper
          and Row.

MILLAN, Robert I.
   1955   "A Voice Out of a Cloud," *The Missionary Standard,* L,
          10:5.

   1969   Interview with author, May 27, 1969.

MISSIONARY INFORMATION BUREAU
   1964   "First Service Questionnaire," Sao Paulo (in the files
          of Missions Advanced Research and Communication Center,
          World Vision, Monrovia, California).

   1967   "The Statistical Missionary Image." Sao Paulo, MIB
          (Occasional Paper 10, May, 1967).

   1968   *Protestant Missions in Brasil: MIB/MARC Directory of
          Non-Catholic Christian Missionary Groups.* Monrovia,
          California, Missions Advanced Research and Communica-
          tion Center.

MISSIONARY RESEARCH LIBRARY and MISSIONS ADVANCED RESEARCH AND
          COMMUNICATION
   1968   *North American Protestant Ministries Overseas.* Waco,
          Texas, Word Books.

NEIL, Stephen Charles
   1964   *A History of Christian Missions.* Harmondsworth, Peli-
          can.

NEVES, Mario
   1955   *Meio Seculo (Polianteia do Cincocentenario do Presbi-
          terianismo no Estado do Espirito Santo).* Sao Paulo,
          Casa Editora Presbiteriana.

NEW TESTAMENT MISSIONARY UNION
   1969   Letter to author May, 1969.

NIDA, Eugene A.
   1958   "The Relationships of Social Structure to the Problems
          of Evangelism in Latin America," *Practical Anthropology,*
          5:3.

ORIENTAL MISSIONARY SOCIETY, The
   1950 - 1968   *The Missionary Standard.* Glendale, California,
                 The Church Press.

   1964a   "The Brazilian," OMS Field Bulletin.

ORIENTAL MISSIONARY SOCIETY, The
    1967a   *Manual of The Oriental Missionary Society.* Greenwood,
              Indiana.

    1967b   *Constitution of The Oriental Missionary Society.* Green-
              wood, Indiana.

    1967c   *By-Laws of The Oriental Missionary Society.* Greenwood,
              Indiana.

ORR, J. Edwin
    1965   *The Light of the Nations.* Vol. 8 of Advance of Chris-
             tianity: The Nineteenth Century. Grand Rapids, Wil-
             liam B. Eerdmans Publishing Company.

    1967   Unpublished lecture notes taken by the author in class.

OVERSEAS CRUSADES
    1968   *Handbook of Principles and Policies.* Palo Alto, Cali-
             fornia.

PEARSON, Benjamin H.
    1951   "God's Open Door in Brazil," *The Missionary Standard,*
             L, 11:5,16.

    1953   "Foundation Stones in Brazil," *The Missionary Standard,*
             LII, 4:7.

    1953a   "The Lord Will Do Wonders Among You," *The Missionary
             Standard,*LII, 8:4,10.

    1955   "Building in Brazil," *The Missionary Standard,* LIV,
             7:4.

    1961   *The Vision Lives: A Profile of Mrs. Charles E. Cowman.*
             Grand Rapids, Zondervan Publishing House.

    1967   Interview with author, May 13, 1967.

PIERSON, Arthur T., ed.
    1901   *The Missionary Review of the World.* New York, Funk
    1902   and Wagnalls Co.
    1906
    1907

PIERSON, Delvan C., ed.
    1925   *The Missionary Review of the World.* New York, Funk
             and Wagnalls Co. (October) 760.

READ, William R.
1965   *New Patterns of Church Growth in Brazil.* Grand Rapids,
        William B. Eerdmans Publishing Company.

1968   "The Scope of Strategy Planning for Latin America,"
        Evangelical Missions Quarterly, (Winter) 110-116.

READ, William R. and BENNETT, Charles
1969   "Urban Explosions: The Challenge in Latin America,"
        *World Vision Magazine,*Vol. 13, 6:6-11.

READ, William R., MONTERROSO, Victor M. and JOHNSON, Harmon A.
1969   *Latin American Church Growth.* Grand Rapids, William
        B. Eerdmans Publishing Company.

SARGINSON, Charles R.
1967   Letter to William R. Read, May 10, 1967.

SCHURZ, William Lytle
1961   *Brazil, The Infinite Country.* New York, E. P. Dutton
        & Co.

SEAMANDS, John T.
1966   "What McGavran's Church Growth Thesis Means," *Evangel-
        ical Missions Quarterly,* (Fall) 21-31.

SOUZA, Eygdio do Camara, and NAMM, Major Benjamin H.
1944   *Post-War Problems of Brazil.* New York, Research Bureau
        for Post-War Economics of the Latin American Economic
        Institute.

TANAAMI, Kozo
1967   Interview with author, June 10, 1967.

TAYLOR, Clyde W. and COGGINS, Wade T., eds.
1961   *Protestant Missions in Latin America: A Statistical
        Survey.* Washington, D. C., Evangelical Foreign Mis-
        sions Association.

TAYLOR, Howard and Mrs.
1943   *Hudson Taylor and the China Inland Mission: The Growth
        of a Work of God.* Philadelphia, The China Inland
        Mission.

TIPPETT, Alan R.
1966   "Church Growth or Else!" *World Vision Magazine,* (Feb-
        ruary) 12-13,28.

1967   *Solomon Islands Christianity.* New York, Friendship
        Press.

TIPPETT, Alan R.
    1969   *Verdict Theology in Missionary Theory.* Lincoln, Illi-
            nois, Lincoln Christian College Press.

UNEVANGELIZED FIELDS MISSION
    1966   Report to CGRILA. (Typewritten).

WAGLEY, Charles
    1963   *An Introduction to Brazil.* New York, Columbia Univer-
            sity Press.

    1968   *Latin American Traditions.* New York, Columbia Univer-
            sity Press.

WAGNER, C. Peter
    1968   "A Preliminary Study of the Origin and Growth of the
            Protestant Church in Bolivia." An unpublished M. A.
            thesis, Fuller Theological Seminary.

WILEY, William T.
    1965   Form sent to CGRILA from South American Indian Mission.

    1967   Form sent to CGRILA from South American Indian Mission,
            June 30, 1967.

WILLEMS, Emilio
    1967   *Followers of the New Faith.* Nashville, Tennessee, Van-
            derbuilt University Press.

WILLIAMS, Robert S.
    n.d.   Form sent to CGRILA from Brazil Gospel Fellowship Mis-
            sion.

WINTER, Ralph D.
    1969   "The Anatomy of the Christian Mission," *Evangelical
            Missions Quarterly,* (Winter) 74-89.

    1969   Interview with author, September 20, 1969.

WOLFF, Orville
    1967   Letter to author, March 16, 1967.

    1969   Interview with author, July 21, 1969.

WORLDWIDE EVANGELIZATION CRUSADE
    1969   Letter to author, May, 1969.

WYTHE, George
    1949   *Brazil an Expanding Economy.* New York, Twentieth Cen-
            tury Fund.

YUASA, Key
   1968   "Churches in Minority Situation: The Brazilian Case."
            Printed report for "Ecumenical Review," Cuernavaca,
            Mexico, CIDOC.

William Carey Library
PUBLICATIONS

Africa

PEOPLES OF SOUTHWEST ETHIOPIA, by A. R. Tippett,Ph.D.
A recent, penetrating evaluation by a professional anthropologist of the cultural complexities
faced by Peace Corps workers and missionaries in a
rapidly changing intersection of African states.
1970: 320 pp, $3.95. ISBN 0-87808-103-8

PROFILE FOR VICTORY: NEW PROPOSALS FOR MISSIONS IN
ZAMBIA, by Max Ward Randall.
*"In a remarkably objective manner the author
has analyzed contemporary political, social educational and religious trends, which demand a re-
examination of traditional missionary methods and
the creation of daring new strategies...his con-
clusions constitute a challenge for the future of
Christian missions, not only in Zambia, but around
the world."*
1970: 224 pp, Cloth, $3.95. ISBN 0-87808-403-7

THE CHURCH OF THE UNITED BRETHREN OF CHRIST IN
SIERRA LEONE, by Emmett D. Cox, Executive Secretary,
United Brethren in Christ Board of Missions.
A readable account of the relevant historical,
demographic and anthropological data as they relate
to the development of the United Brethren in Christ
Church in the Mende and Creole communities. Includes a reformation of objectives.
1970: 184 pp, $2.95. ISBN 0-87808-301-4

APPROACHING THE NUER OF AFRICA THROUGH THE OLD
TESTAMENT, by Ernest A. McFall.
The author examines in detail the simila-
rities between the Nuer and the Hebrews of the Old
Testament and suggests a novel Christian approach
that does not make initial use of the New Testament.
1970: 104 pp, 8 1/2 x 11, $1.95.
ISBN 0-87808-310-3

Asia

TAIWAN: MAINLINE VERSUS INDEPENDENT CHURCH GROWTH, A STUDY IN CONTRASTS, by Allen J. Swanson.

A provocative comparison between the older, historical Protestant churches in Taiwan and the new indigenous Chinese churches; suggests staggering implications for missions everywhere that intend to promote the development of truly indigenous expressions of Christianity.

1970: 216 pp, $2.95.   ISBN 0-87808-404-5

NEW PATTERNS FOR DISCIPLING HINDUS: THE NEXT STEP IN ANDHRA PRADESH, INDIA, by B.V. Subbamma.

Proposes the development of a Christian movement that is as well adapted culturally to the Hindu tradition as the present movement is to the Harijan tradition. Nothing could be more crucial for the future of 400 million Hindus in India today.

1970: 212 pp, $3.45. ISBN 0-87808-306-5

GOD'S MIRACLES: INDONESIAN CHURCH GROWTH, by Ebbie C. Smith, Th.D.

The fascinating details of the penetration of Christianity into the Indonesian archipelago make for intensely interesting reading, as the anthropological context and the growth of the Christian movement are highlighted.

1970: 224 pp, $3.45. ISBN 0-87808-302-2

NOTES ON CHRISTIAN OUTREACH IN A PHILIPPINE COMMUNITY, by Marvin K. Mayers, Ph.D.

The fresh observations of an anthropologist coming from the outside provide a valuable, however preliminary, check list of social and historical factors in the context of missionary endeavors in a Tagalog province.

1970: 71 pp, 8 1/2 x 11, $1.45. ISBN 0-87808-104-6

Latin America

THE PROTESTANT MOVEMENT IN BOLIVIA, by C. Peter Wagner.

An excitingly-told account of the gradual build-up and present vitality of Protestantism. A cogent analysis of the various subcultures and the organizations working most effectively, including a striking evaluation of Bolivia's momentous Evangelism-in-Depth year and the possibilities of Evangelism-in-Depth for other parts of the world.

1970: 264 pp, $3.95. ISBN 0-87808-402-9

LA SERPIENTE Y LA PALOMA, by Manuel Gaxiola.

The impressive success story of the Apostolic Church of Mexico, (an indigenous denomination that never had the help of any foreign missionary), told by a professional scholar now the director of research for that church. (Spanish)

1970: 200 pp, $2.95. ISBN 0-87808-802-4

THE EMERGENCE OF A MEXICAN CHURCH: THE ASSOCIATE REFORMED PRESBYTERIAN CHURCH OF MEXICO, by James Erskine Mitchell.

Tells the ninety-year story of the Associate Reformed Presbyterian Mission in Mexico, the trials and hardships as well as the bright side of the work. Eminently practical and helpful regarding the changing relationship of mission and church in the next decade.

1970: 184 pp, $2.95. ISBN 0-87808-303-0

FRIENDS IN CENTRAL AMERICA, by Paul C. Enyart.

This book describes the results of faithful and effective labors of the California Friends Yearly Meeting, giving an analysis of the growth of one of the most virile, national evangelical churches in Central America, comparing its growth to other evangelical churches in Guatemala, Honduras, and El Salvador.

1970: 224 pp, $3.45. ISBN 0-87808-405-3

Europe

THE CHALLENGE FOR EVANGELICAL MISSIONS TO EUROPE: A SCANDINAVIAN CASE STUDY, by Hilkka Malaska.

Graphically presents the state of Christianity in Scandinavia with an evaluation of the pros and cons and possible contributions that existing or additional Evangelical missions can make in Europe today.

1970: 192 pp, $2.95. ISBN 0-87808-308-1

THE PROTESTANT MOVEMENT IN ITALY: ITS PROGRESS, PROBLEMS, AND PROSPECTS, by Roger Hedlund.

A carefully wrought summary of preliminary data; perceptively develops issues faced by Evangelical Protestants in all Roman Catholic areas of Europe. Excellent graphs.

1970: 266 pp, $3.95. ISBN 0-87808-307-3

U.S.A.

THE YOUNG LIFE CAMPAIGN AND THE CHURCH, by Warren Simandle.

If 70 per cent of young people drop out of the church between the ages of 12 and 20, is there room for a nationwide Christian organization working on high school campuses? After a quarter of a century, what is the record of Young Life and how has its work with teens affected the church? *"A careful analysis based on a statistical survey; full of insight and challenging proposals for both Young Life and the church."*

1970: 216 pp, $3.45. ISBN 0-87808-304-9

THE RELIGIOUS DIMENSION IN SPANISH LOS ANGELES: A PROTESTANT CASE STUDY, by Clifton L. Holland.

A through analysis of the origin, development and present extent of this vital, often unnoticed element in Southern California.

1970: 304 pp, $3.95. ISBN 0-87808-309-X

General

THEOLOGICAL EDUCATION BY EXTENSION, edited by Ralph D. Winter, Ph.D.

A husky handbook on a new approach to the education of pastoral leadership for the church. Gives both theory and practice and the exciting historical development in Latin America of the *"Largest non-governmental voluntary educational development project in the world today."* Ted Ward, Prof. of Education, Michigan State University.

1969: 648 pp, Library Buckram $7.95, Kivar $4.95. ISBN 0-87808-101-1

THE CHURCH GROWTH BULLETIN, VOL. I-V, edited by Donald A. McGavran, Ph.D.

The first five years of issues of a now-famous bulletin which probes past foibles and present opportunities facing the 100,000 Protestant and Catholic missionaries in the world today. No periodical edited for this audience has a larger readership.

1969: 408 pp, Library Buckram $6.95, Kivar $4.45. ISBN 0-87808-701-X

CHURCH GROWTH THROUGH EVANGELISM-IN-DEPTH, by
Malcolm R. Bradshaw.

*"Examines the history of Evangelism-in-Depth
and other total mobilization approaches to evangelism. Also presents concisely the 'Church
Growth' approach to mission and proposes a
wedding between the two...a great blessing to the
church at work in the world."* WORLD VISION
MAGAZINE.

1969: 152 pp, $2.45. ISBN 0-87808-401-0

THE TWENTY FIVE UNBELIEVABLE YEARS, 1945-1969, by
Ralph D. Winter, Ph.D.

A terse, exciting analysis of the most significant transition in human history in this millenium
and its impact upon the Christian movement. *"Packed
with insight and otherwise unobtainable statistical
data...a brilliant piece of work."* C. Peter Wagner.

1970: 120 pp, $1.95. ISBN 0-87808-102-X

EL SEMINARIO DE EXTENSION: UN MANUAL, by James H.
Emery, F. Ross Kinsler, Louise J. Walker, Ralph D.
Winter.

Gives the reasons for the extension approach to
the training of ministers, as well as the concrete,
practical details of establishing and operating
such a program. A Spanish translation of the third
section of *THEOLOGICAL EDUCATION BY EXTENSION*.

1969: 256 pp, $3.45. ISBN 0-87808-801-6

ABOUT THE WILLIAM CAREY LIBRARY

William Carey is widely considered the "Father of Modern Missions" partly because many people think he was the first Protestant missionary. Even though there was a trickle of others before him, he deserves very special honor for many valiant accomplishments in his heroic career, but most particularly because of three things he did before he ever left England, things no one else in history before him had combined together:

1) he had an authentic,personal, evangelical passion to serve God and acknowledged this as obligating him to fulfill God's interests in the redemption of all men on the face of the earth.

2) he actually proposed a structure for the accomplishment of that aim - he did indeed, more than anyone else, set off the movement among Protestants for the creation of "voluntary societies" for foreign missions, and

3) he added to all of this a strategic literary and research achievement: shaky those statistics may have been, but he put together the very best possible estimate of the number of unreached peoples in every part of the globe, and summarized previous, relatively ineffective attempts to reach them. His burning conclusion was that existing efforts were not proportional to the opportunities and the scope of Christian obligation in Mission.

Today, a little over 150 years later, the situation is not wholly different. In the past five years, for example, experienced missionaries from all corners of the earth (53 countries) have brought to the Fuller School of World Mission and Institute of Church Growth well over 800 years of missionary experience. Twenty-six scholarly books have resulted from the research of faculty and students. The best statistics available have at times been shaky -though far superior to Carey's - but vision has been clear and the mandate is as urgent as ever. The printing press is still the right arm of Christians active in the Christian world mission.

The William Carey Library is a new publishing house dedicated to books related to this mission. There are many publishers, both secular and religious, that occasionally publish books of this kind. We believe there is no other devoted exclusively to the production and distribution of books for career missionaries and their home churches.

ABOUT THE AUTHOR

In 1964 Fred E. Edwards was commissioned a missionary to
Brazil with the Oriental Missionary Society. There he served
for two and one half years. For more than a year of this time
he was actively involved in a church-planting ministry as Director of the Good News Crusade. Together with a team of Brazilian
lay evangelists he planted five congregations in the north of
the Brazilian state of Parana. Coupled to his role of church
planter was that of professor in the Londrina Bible Institute
and Seminary of Londrina, Parana.

Mr. Edwards attended Asbury College and Asbury Theological
Seminary at Wilmore, Kentucky where he received the B.A. and
B.D. degrees in 1959 and 1963. More recently he earned his M.A.
at the School of World Missions and Institute of Church Growth,
Fuller Theological Seminary, Pasadena, California while pastor-
ing the Faith Missionary Church of Pomona, California.